Sexy Boss:

How Female Entrepreneurs are Beating the Big Boys While Changing the Rule Book for Success, Money and Even Sex and How You Can Too!

Heather Havenwood

Sexy Boss:
How Female Entrepreneurs are Beating the Big Boys While Changing the Rule Book for Success, Money and Even Sex and How You Can Too!

Copyright © 2012, 2016 by Heather Havenwood

ISBN-10: 0-9894663-5-3
ISBN-13: 978-0-9894663-5-6

Printed in USA

Dedication

Coach Kym Dolcimascolo, Mentor Joe Sugarman and my mother Julie Hogaboom.

Heather Havenwood

Table of Contents

Foreword

Get ready for a revolution. Women are quickly learning how to build and grow a business and most interestingly, how to compete with the big boys.

The playing field is now a level one for women. And if you fail to recognize this, you'll be putting yourself at a great disadvantage. Let me explain.

Women who enroll in law schools throughout the country now outnumber men applicants. Thanks to the Internet, women are able to use their skills to start on-line businesses and build very successful companies—many overnight. Yes, woman are slowly realizing the power they have and expressing their potential in ways that take advantage of their business skills and interestingly, their sexuality.

In Sexy Boss, Heather Havenwood covers the world of women and sex and the important role they play in running and building a business. "It's OK to be sexy," says Havenwood, "It's part of the basket full of advantages available to women today that many don't even realize.

In Sexy Boss, Havenwood relates the emotional rollercoaster ride she went through to meet the expectations of others in her desire to be productive and successful. Her stories are riveting. Many of these stories teach life lessons you won't find anywhere else. Many show how a simple attitude correction can change your life.

If you are a woman in business or if you want to start a business, you must read this book. First, it's unlike any other business book. Why? Because it gives you all the tools you'll need as a woman to succeed and prosper in what was previously only a man's world.

Secondly, it unleashes the power you have as a woman that you might not realize you even had. And finally, it is a compelling read—one that will keep you reading page after page unable to put down. I firmly believe in the potential of women in business and I'm thrilled to have this opportunity to support that potential in this foreword. It is my sense that many lives will be changed for the better as a result of Havenwood's book.

Joseph Sugarman
Founder and Chairman
BluBlocker Corporation

Introduction

From Bankruptcy to Sexy Boss

Hi,

My name is Heather Havenwood and I am a Sexy Boss.

I wasn't always a Sexy Boss, however...

After being spit out by the corporate world and growing tired of sales jobs that paid well but left me empty, I launched my own real estate business at the tender age of 25.

I was kicking butt and taking names. It quickly became a 7-figure company that I operated out of my home with two other partners, whom I trusted completely to manage the money and financial side of the business.

Things were going great -- amazing actually -- until one day I was hit with the biggest shock of my life. I had been away at a weekend seminar, and arrived back at my home, only to see that one of my partners and all his stuff was suddenly gone. Worse yet, ALL of my bank accounts were emptied...I was literally wiped out.

I was not only devastated, I was in big time financial trouble. My whole life, including my mortgage, and everything else, revolved around this business.

I had nothing.

It wasn't long before I was forced to declare bankruptcy and give up my home. Flat broke and bankrupt, both my personal and business credit were shattered.

Then Came The Epiphany...

At that moment, I made a clear decision to NOT re-enter the workforce my tail between my legs, but instead, to create my life on my own terms.

No more fucking around, no more excuses. I thought, *"I'm GOING to be the boss of my life...I WILL succeed,"* and for the first time in my life, I totally meant it.

It was during that time that the principles behind Sexy Boss began to emerge and be revealed to me. I used them in my own life, transforming not only my career, but also my income, my relationships... even the way I felt about myself.

I emerged as a Sexy Boss -- a woman powerfully in command of every part of her life. I launched my own businesses, found love, competed in fitness competitions, and much much more. I was on fire and others took notice. Soon, I was invited to speak and share everything I had learned, and exactly how the process I discovered could help women.

Which brings us to today. My mission is to champion women everywhere to awaken the Sexy Boss within and realize their greatness. *And do it with attitude.*

Because being the boss is sexy!

Be You! Be Real! Be Sexy Boss,

Heather Havenwood

P.S. Take the Sexy Boss Pledge and retrieve your free copy of the Sexy Boss Manifesto at www.SexyBossInc.com

P.P.S. As a Bonus for your purchase of Sexy Boss – FREE bonus content has been reserved, exclusively for you! Claim it by going to www.sexybossinc.com/book_bonus

Chapter 1

Time to Wake the F$#@! Up

"A stumbling block to the pessimist is a stepping stone to the optimist." -- Eleanor Roosevelt

This is a wakeup call.

Not because you're weak or limited, but because you're infinitely powerful.

If you're like most people, you're bought into a narrative, a set of limiting stories and excuses that largely defines what you believe you can and can't do.

And it's total BS.

It's not you. Not the REAL YOU, at least.

This chapter is all about helping you wake up to the truth about who you are (a Sexy Boss!), what's holding you back, and how to break free once and for all.

It's Easy to Feel Like a Victim

We've all had bad things happen to us. Some worse than others. As you'll see later in the book, I personally had some pretty unfortunate things done to me – especially on a financial level.

I'm not here to judge or evaluate what's happened to you.

That is the past.
The only thing I care about is helping you move forward.

Because the society we live in makes it very convenient to feel and present ourselves as a victim.

And no, I'm not talking about poverty or welfare – I don't want to get into a political debate.

I'm about how common it is to feel like a victim on an everyday personal level.

Feel Sorry for Me, Please

Have you ever been late somewhere?

You probably felt bad about it. And then, at the same time, you maybe, offered an excuse to the person why you were late to meeting.

"The traffic was terrible."
"I was waiting for my ride."
"The alarm didn't go off."
"I had to pick my friend up and he wasn't ready."

These are just a few of the huge number of excuses that are possible and frequent when someone is late. They sound different, but they all have one thing in common: The denial of your power.

Each time you present an excuse like this, you are denying your power.

It's subtle, and I'm not saying that it destroys us.

But with each excuse, we are essentially saying "this outside circumstance or person is more powerful than I am."

It's easy to blame being late on something outside of yourself. Then you're not responsible and don't have to feel as bad to the person you're communicating with. This happens all the time.

However, what we don't realize is that these little denials of our power add up.

Over time, they create a pattern of making outside circumstances and other people more powerful than we are. By inviting others to feel sorry or take pity on us in moments of need – rather than owning our results in life, we slowly strangle our personal power.

Responsibility = Power

The first step in moving away from victimhood and toward power is becoming fully responsible.

That means fully owning the results of your life, every single day. Even the little things!

In other words… if you're late. It's not because of traffic, it's because you didn't leave early enough. Or you didn't check the traffic report. Or you didn't plan appropriately.

On a deeper level, if we are ever late, it's because *we weren't fully committed to being on time.*

That will be one of the biggest aha's of your life, I guarantee you.

Because it doesn't just apply to being late or on time, it applies to EVERYTHING.

The Infinite Power of Commitment

In life, we don't get what we "deserve"… we tend to get what we are truly committed to.

If you're 100% committed to being fit and healthy… you will be.

If you're 100% committed to being wealthy and doing whatever it takes (ethically I hope!)… you will get there.

If you're 100% committed to finding love and being in an amazing relationship, you'll get that too.

This isn't a "rah rah, you can do it!" message. Actually, I'm here to tell you why you're NOT doing or getting what you want.

Because virtually every time we want something but are not currently experiencing that thing in our life, it's because our commitment is not 100%.

Sure, some people may be fortunate – they manage to get things they are not fully committed to. But don't point to examples like a "trust fund baby" or the genetically gifted athlete as examples of people who "got lucky".

Because if the privileged child wants to someday start an ambitious business or the gifted athlete wants to be a world champion, his result will also come down to the level of his or her commitment. Period.

There are no exceptions to this rule.

Want to Know What You're Committed To? Just Look Around!

The results in your life – whether it's health, wealth, career, love or anything else are ALWAYS a direct reflection of your commitment.

So if you want to know what you're committed to – just look around.

You may be committed to greatness in some areas but not others.

You may be committed to things you didn't even realize!

For instance, if you watch TV religiously every day instead if investing time into a business – you're probably more committed to watching TV than being independently wealthy.

I'm not saying you are doing that, it's just an example.

It's important to wake up, become more aware, and evaluate what's going on in your life and SEE how your commitment is reflected in the results you're getting.

The more clearly you see this, the more powerful you'll feel.

Actually, you might be angry in the beginning – once you begin to see the truth.

It's infuriating when we see that we're more committed to things that fundamentally don't make us very happy, while we ignore things that are much more important and meaningful.

And we all do it. From the homeless person to the greatest CEO's and presidents.
The difference is how much you're able to see that, own it by taking responsibility, and then move in a new direction.

Before you can do that, you should ask yourself the question…

Are You Afraid of Full Commitment?

Most people are. I was. And sometimes still find myself shying away from giving 100% to something that I really want, deep down.

Why is that? Why is it so common for us to avoid full commitment?

I believe that it's fear – the fear of what failure says about us.

If you never go fully in, we never fully expose ourselves. That way, if we fail, it doesn't mean that inherently we're not good enough. It just means that we didn't fully try.

100% commitment means completely putting ourselves on the line, and that's scary. If we fail in that case, we think it means that we're not good enough – or worse, that something is wrong with us.

Which is of course, absolute nonsense, but it's what we believe.

In reality, being 100% committed – and failure – are necessary to achieve anything great.

Some of the greatest achievers this world has ever known have literally failed their way to success. The difference was that, due to their extraordinary level of commitment, they never stopped.

My dear friend, Joe Sugarman, said to me once "Heather, I am successful because I have been willing to fail and I have failed more than I have succeeded."
Joe and others never made excuses, asked others to feel sorry for them, or blamed their circumstances on the failure. That's the difference.

Be Ruthlessly Honest With Yourself

A big part of this process is becoming brutally – if not ruthlessly – honest with yourself.

Because we have become masters of deception.

Again, look at how we've tricked ourselves into thinking that we're victims, and that other people or circumstances have power over our lives.

In reality, it's insane! Yet we all do it or have done it. It's so easy to deceive ourselves and then to deceive others in order to receive their pity.

So seeing this, again, it's imperative that you be 100% honest. Don't buy into your own excuses. If you're overweight, don't blame bed genetics or the fact that your parents didn't teach you good habits. Own it.

If you're broke, don't blame your boss or your school or the government. Own it.

See that you can have anything you're truly committed to. Commit 100% to being healthy, or rich, or anything you want – and you'll have it.

It's really simple.

You have the power, but that power can only shine through and into your life when we stop burying it under the weight of victim thinking.

Wake Up Your Sexy Boss Within

Throughout this book, we'll continue to define what a Sexy Boss is – and how you can become one.

However, the first and most important step is right here in this chapter. It's waking up.

It's about no longer letting yourself use inauthentic scripts and stories others have written – whether it's a small thing like being late, or a big thing like why you're not where you want to be with your career or finances.

Start catching your excuses and learn to take full responsibility for the all the results that experience in your life.

Being a Sexy Boss – and waking up to that – can and will help you do extraordinary things.

But it's up to you to get the process started now.

Don't wait! "Tomorrow" is just another lie we tell ourselves.

Look around, take responsibility for your entire life, every part of your life – and then use that power to seize what you want.

Get going -- right now!

A Sexy Boss doesn't wait for things to be given to her – she makes what she wants happen in her life. Period.

This book will help you get started – the rest is up to you.

Final Thoughts From a Sexy Boss

It's time to wake the F$#@! up!! Look around. Take inventory of your life. It's easy to feel like a victim, but it's just as easy to recognize your power.

Your power lies in your level of commitment. Any result in your life – positive or negative -- is a reflection of how committed you are. By eliminating excuses and committed completely to what you want, you become a Sexy Boss with unlimited power to make things happen.

Chapter 2

Taking Total Ownership Over Your Thoughts

"Fun is not defined as the absence of challenging circumstances, but as the absence of anger about them." – **Neale Donald Walsch**

You may not be able to fully control your thoughts, but you can take responsibility for them.

That's what it means to "own" your thoughts. To acknowledge that you have the power to influence and direct your thinking and the focus of your mind.

In this chapter, we're going to discover how you can reclaim your power in this key area – to be fully aware of your thoughts, how they affect you, and how you can stop being a victim of limited thinking.

And yes, this applies to you as a woman. Sometimes we're given a free pass because "we're just a woman" or "it's that time of the month"… and other bullshit excuses.

Because as a strong Sexy Boss woman, you're every bit as responsible for what happens in your mind as anyone else – maybe more so. Because you're even more self-aware than most people.

But enough of the theoretical. Let's take this to a more practical level, beginning with something called…

The Power of Muscle-Testing

The muscle test is a process where one places their hand out, while another person tries to move their arm down, and the first person resists it. They ask the person, "Hold your hand still, hold your arm still, I'm going to push, resist me," and they usually can resist with a fair amount of strength. Next they'll say, "Now think of something you really love."

Now when I first tried this demonstration, I thought of my dog, Lady, the love of my life. Seriously, Lady is amazing. I love her so much! She gives me all kinds of joy.

Nobody messes with Lady, or they answer to me.

So when the person tried to push my arm down while I was thinking of Lady, it was strong. Really strong!

After that, the person said, "Think of the catastrophe that's happened. Say, for example, the massacre that occurred in Denver, where all those people that were killed." The moment she said that, my arm became weak. She did it again. Said "Think of Lady," arm strong. "Think of the massacre," arm weak.

It didn't matter how much my brain said, "Hold strong." It didn't matter. I tried, but I just couldn't hold it.

So what does this mean?

Obviously, when we do a poor job of managing your focus and you give in to negativity -- negative thoughts, negative images – it weakens us. Not in a theoretical or imaginary way. But quite literally, even physically, in our muscles.

Can you imagine areas or patterns of thought that might be weakening you now?

When you put any form of extended attention on something negative, you begin to make it real for yourself. And you are 100% responsible for that. You and you alone.

It's not the fault of anyone else, because only you have the ability to change and control your point of focus. Harp on something negative, and it will take your power away. It takes your energy away. It just sucks it right out. Period.

Of course, what's negative for one person might be positive for another. There's no strict set of rules – just as there's always two sides to everything.

Which brings us to the importance of the energetic or emotional association we have with specific thoughts.

When we talk about positive or negative, it's not necessarily about right versus wrong. When I think of my dog, Lady, I get strong. But when you see the same dog, Lady, you might not get as strong. You like her, but the strength and positive vibration of my association creates the strength I experienced in the test.

Think about a political debate. One might be a Democratic, and therefore get strong when thinking about Barack Obama or Bill Clinton. It's not necessarily that the person or thing being thought about is bad or good.

What matters is the *emotion and feelings* we associate with it.

In this sense, the impact of a particular thought is personal and subject. And it's up to you to feel and know whether your association with something creates positivity and strength, or negativity and weakness.

So how does this relate to being a Sexy Boss?

Focus Exclusively On Thoughts You Have *Positive Associations* With

Obviously, your thinking affects you in countless ways. In fact, virtually every situation you encounter, whether business or personal, is impacted by your thoughts and the corresponding feelings you associate with it.
Note: We women are often criticized for being "emotional" or having lots of "feeling"… but what I'm talking about regarding associations is universal. It's not about being a man or woman, and actually – as a Sexy Boss, you're going to learn how to use everything you feel to your advantage.

This is why awareness is so important.

Because the truth is, whether we realize it or not, we are always associating emotions with thoughts… and then choosing what we focus on. The more aware we are of our thoughts and how they are affecting us, the more we take ownership of our creative power.

For example, imagine you find yourself in a situation (such as a new job) that may not be your ideal situation. You could bitch and complain, which is what most people do. Most would whine while internally labeling this as a "negative" situation, but then you'll be weakening yourself.

And that will be 100% your choice.

On the other hand, even though it's not your ideal situation, you could choose to label the situation positively as an "opportunity" – which would in turn cause you to feel stronger and more empowered about your situation.

Again, you "create" either way – but what you create, whether constructive or destructive, depends on you and the choices you make.
Yes, you *always* have a choice.

And it's not just things or situations, this also pertains to people you encounter or those currently in your life. If you look at a person and you go, "Oh my god, look at that horrible, scruffy, low-life, bottom-feeding person over there," that's all negative. You'll feel weak when you see them, or in their presence.

Whether you want to admit it or not, that takes <u>your</u> energy away. Own your thoughts and <u>your</u> speaking! They affect you every moment of every day. You can be the passenger, or you can be the driver, the choice is yours.

Because you could see a scruffy homeless person and then choose to see the divinity that person. And if you did, you'd be consciously choose to empower yourself and strengthen yourself.

Sexy Boss Exercise

Here is an exercise that will assist you in thinking newly like a Sexy Boss in life. Think of something that annoys you - daily. Something that bugs you or you complain about on a daily basis. Traffic? Your Spouse? Your Kids? Your Job?

Write the complaint on an actual piece of paper. For example: "I do not like sitting in traffic everyday going to work." OR "It is annoying to me that my spouse never picks up his clothes off the bedroom floor."

GET VERY SPECIFIC. Write down the specific complaint.

Next, what is one thing that you can be grateful about that? One little thing that you can see gratitude within that person or situation.

Example: I can be grateful for the car that I have to drive me in this traffic. Or I am grateful for the radio show that I listen to daily on my drive.

Or

I am grateful for my spouse mowing the lawn last week. Or I am grateful for the maid that is coming this Monday to help me with the laundry.

Again, we always have the choice. I can't say that enough.

In fact, the power of choice is a big reason why Eastern spiritual traditions like Zen put such a tremendous emphasis on awareness. Because awareness of our thoughts and how they impact us gives us more choice over how we react – and therefore more freedom.

That's why it's critical for you to be aware of the feelings and emotions you associate with the thinking going on in your head. Because only when you're aware can you consciously choose to change or create something new.

This way, you become self-expansive – which is a core part of the empowerment process we'll cover throughout this book.
Focusing on positive thoughts is a way to deliberately, a way of reclaiming your ability to create the reality you desire.

Being a Sexy Boss of one's self, of yourself, no matter what the situation is, no matter if it's what I call a "hurricane" around you, is largely about being *self-expansive.*

By connecting to what's positive and makes you feel genuinely good, you are connecting to your higher self, higher source, to higher energy, and you are creating.

You are stepping into your power. That's what sexy boss is all about.

It really is a choice. I don't mean that you have to put on rose-colored glasses and live in fantasy land, where everything is wonderful.

You can be honest when something is wrong, or feels bad. The point is, do you choose to wallow in that negative vibration and let it define you, or to shift your focus and consciously move in the direction you want?

Because being a Sexy Boss is about always choosing to move forward, and up – no matter what. You always have the choice.

Heather's Sexy Boss Saying: "Onward and Upward!"

In every chapter, I will be sharing a story.

From Bankrupt to Successful Sexy Boss

I'm going to share my story of a hardship for me that was something that I thought I'd never go through. That was personal bankruptcy and foreclosure.

I want to give you my life context.

The world for me when I grew up in high school, even in junior high, was I had this complete confidence that I was going to be this very successful woman. It came from a place of anger. It didn't come from a place of creation. It came from a place of chaos, anger, and fighting. I had to fight my way.

That was my thorn in my side: I had to fight for everything that I had. I was willing to fight whoever was in the way.

I was in foster care by the time I was 16, 17. I spent my last senior year in high school in foster care. Then I left. I really was on my own ever since.

Starting in college, I didn't have what I'd call "a place to go home to". You know how people go home during the holidays or they go home for the weekend? There really wasn't that for me. I began to be very defensive and isolated.

However, there was also strong part of me developing. I became a very outgoing, "I can get it done" person, during this time. I developed a strong, successful, and a very large "I don't need you" attitude that made me very independent.

By the time I was 24-25, I had been working for a company for five years, a Fortune 500 company. I was an outside sales rep for them at an extremely young age. My co-workers were in their forties, and I was extremely young. I fought every day. I fought to be number one.

But the drawback to the power I'd developed was that I didn't care about my co-workers. I didn't care about relationship with my co-workers. I didn't really care about my boss that much. I just cared about those numbers and fighting to be number one and compete.

And so I did. I was number one out of 10,000 reps across the country in really what they call a B territory, it wasn't a large territory. I became number one even though I was in the B territory. I overcame the odds via sheer determination and fight.

Unfortunately, as soon as I got that medal or as soon as I got that acknowledgement from the company, everything went downhill from there. All of a sudden, I was extremely depressed. I left the company. And within six months, I was in a place where I was mentally really down.

At that point in my life, I didn't how to "be" any other way, but to fight. So I tried to fight those feelings and fight that depression and fight that sense of feeling upset. I continually fought those feelings of not good enough. I had no idea on how to shift that or to shift my association and focus toward something I wanted, in the direction of self-expansion. I had no tools to do that.

Within about a few years, I moved to Florida from Texas and I got a new job. I traveled around the country, speaking. I spoke on real estate investing. During that time, I learned skills on speaking. I learned skills on how to present and I learned about promotion, self-promotion -- many skills that I use today.

In that time, I bought my first home before the age of 30.

I was extremely proud of myself. I didn't ask for help on the down payment. I did it myself. I did all the negotiations. I bought the house without a realtor. I bought the house direct from a for sale-by-owner. I did all the contracts myself. I found a title company and I closed it.

And then, one day, December 5, 2005, I had been building a company, an online marketing company, we've done very well in the first year, about $1 million in sales. I was running it out of my home with a co-worker that I had brought in.

So I came home that day after being in a seminar, my co-worker wasn't there and something was off. Within hours, I found that the website had been moved, all the bank accounts had been emptied, the merchant accounts had been moved to different bank accounts, and I was completely locked out of my own company.

I remember that day very vividly – it felt like there was a tornado over my house. There was like a sucking sound over my house, like everything was being sucked out. Almost like from Wizard of Oz where the house is being thrown violently up into the air and away.

I didn't know what to do. I kind of just stopped living. It felt like all the energy of me had been sucked out.

Within about three months, it was clear that I was losing the house because all my money was coming in from the business – and I no longer had cash flow from that business. Within six months -- I still had all the debt from the business and had to make that phone that began with, "Hi, Mr. Bankruptcy Lawyer..." which I don't wish upon anyone.

At this point in my life, I felt this was the one thing in my life that I was fearful of. There were so many things in my life that I wasn't fearful of, like if I got married, got divorced, something like well, my parents got divorced, I've been through that. If I hurt myself or someone attacked me, I always felt that I could attack back.

There were a lot of things in life I just wasn't scared of – traveling around the world by myself, being in hotels by myself, being with different people by myself, knowing that I'll be safe.

There were all kinds of things I wasn't afraid of. Except that one thing, which was financial bankruptcy, there was this heaviness around it.

There's a reason why I'm bringing this up so early in this book. It took me about a year and a half to go through that process. And then another four years to get over it, if not five.

My mental association around the word, "bankruptcy" was so negative for me – it took me years to get over the fact that I'm not a failure and yet a business failed.

Only You Can Direct Your Mind
Toward Positive Associations

This brings up a good point about our associations – often times they are taught to us, and necessarily authentic or inherent in us.

Obviously, nobody wants to be bankrupt. It's pretty universally negative. Still, in my own case, it was especially charged with negativity – perhaps because I had such a "do it myself" and "be strong" attitude. And this was a clear and very public sign of weakness. So for me, bankruptcy was possibly the worst thing I "could be".

By now I hope you see, however, that I was the one giving it that extreme association. It was my responsibility, and only something I could change.

For others, it could be something like divorce – they may have extreme negative feelings about divorce. Others could be the opposite -- when they think of the word "divorce," they think of freedom, they think of release, they think of future.

What's interesting about the word "bankruptcy" on a more factual level, not my personal and social background, is that the definition of word was actually placed into the United States Constitution.

It was placed there because they wanted this country to be based on free market enterprise, and they wanted to be able to have a place where people can build a business – and still be okay if somehow the business failed.

In essence, it was a positive loophole, one that allowed people to take big risks, perhaps fail and not have their lives ruined. Walt Disney went bankrupt, Donald Trump has filed bankruptcy, the list goes on.

As with everything in life, you don't win all the time. Business is like that too. It's a game.

Relationships are like that too -- not all of them are going to end up being a 25-year long happy marriage. There is a beginning, there's a middle and, then, sometimes, there is an end. It could be five years, ten years, 20 years. Same thing with a business. That's what bankruptcy is actually designed for.

There is no reason to beat ourselves up, or perpetuate such deeply negative associations.

I recently read a book called *Monopoly*. It is actually based on the board game. If you look at the game board of Monopoly, on one corner, there's a get out of jail free card.

And on the other side is bankruptcy.

Now in this book, they talked about the game and how the game was created. And why the game was created, based on what they called "perfect capitalist society" – and that if we didn't have bankruptcy, we couldn't have the game of Monopoly, and we couldn't have capitalism.

I'm reminded of a friend of mine that immigrated to the United States from Greece. He and I were talking one night. He says it's a great country because you can try out business ideas, fail and can file for bankruptcy and there's low consequences.

But he said anywhere else in the world, if you tried that, somebody would shoot you because there is no protection. Bankruptcy is protection. He said there in other countries - If you run out of money and you owe people and you can't pay them, they'll just shoot you or you go to jail.

More importantly, the point I want to drive home here is that bankruptcy is just a word. We add the meaning we want to it. I now look at that same word, which used to cause me such pain, and get a massive sense of freedom. It helped prevent me from having to go to jail for the debt even though my partner stole the business, and allowed me to start all over.

What's powerful about this is that now I have this awareness, it doesn't scare me and, there's no negative energy around it anymore. Therefore, it's almost like I'm not attracting it. I've discovered that what you fear most is often what you end up creating.

I feel privileged to know that I have made huge successes in business, and I've also had failures. Both matter. Both are learning experiences.

And this is a big part of being a Sexy Boss. You might have a relationship that worked for many years and then, all of a sudden, it's not working. Or you might have a career that was perfect for you when you're 20, and now you're in a place where it doesn't work anymore for you; it's not the lifestyle you choose now.

Being a Sexy Boss, I feel, is someone who knows that, and chooses her own thoughts no matter what society says you should or shouldn't do. Or should and shouldn't be.

Looking back at the 2012 Olympics, you had Gabby Douglas, the beautiful gymnast and Michael Phelps, now the most decorated Olympian in the world, who had both failed many times.

In Phelps' case, he actually finished 4th in his first race before making a strong comeback and breaking the record.

Yet I guarantee he had the ability to shift his focus and association to something positive, something that uplifted him. Same with Gabby. Being a great gymnast means falling and failing many times before you succeed.

Denial of Choice Makes Us Victims, Affirmation of Choice Makes You Sexy

And it's the same with being a Sexy Boss. It's shutting up – stopping the whining and complaining and other victim narratives. And then consciously choosing your thoughts, choosing more powerful words.

There's a whole story called "Three Feet From Gold." It's a story about a man from the early 1900s who goes out west to find gold. He buys this plot of land. He digs, and digs, and digs but couldn't find anything. Then, somebody else bought the land and bought his old equipment and started where he stopped, and he was three feet away from the gold.

I bring this up, because it ties into this point about your associations and beliefs. Often, when you're able to be aware and shift your focus to positive associations, you're happier and able to persist longer.

And this is true for anyone who succeed at something great. At one point or another, they made the choice to STOP with any victim thinking, and focus on what they want.

And the same goes for you. If you want to be unique and make your mark on the world, you'll need to be radically honest with yourself.

For example, many people are locked into the mindset that they need to go into an office for a 9-5 "job". And yet, that is a limitation – these days there are more opportunities than ever to either start your own business or work remotely. (We'll be talking about both these options later in the book.)

Yet, it comes back to your associations – and your decision to be flexible and shift your focus to something positive.

For example, I have a friend was offered a very desirable job working remotely. He's Florida-based and he was offered a job by a Saudi Arabia company. They would pay for him to move, to live in hotels all over the world for two years and they were going to pay him a large amount of money via 2-year contract, with all kinds of amazing benefits. He said "no" and for the life of me, I couldn't understand why.

He doesn't have kids. He doesn't have a sick mom or something. Why? It's good money. It was full of adventure and travel. It was different.

But the problem was, he just wasn't able to make a positive enough association – the thought of being so far outside the norm was negative to him. So instead, he got a lesser job with a US-based company in Florida and totally sold himself short.

I found that interesting because this particular person had been complaining that in his industry, all the money's been going overseas.

It is going overseas. The companies in his industry are making the most money overseas, especially in India. But he's so adamant that it has to look a certain way that once he got a job for double the salary he was at and it was overseas, where his industry's headed, he wouldn't take it because it was just foreign to him.

So it is a critically important first step to the Sexy Boss process that you're able to be self aware, and to be able to recognize that you're in the driver's seat of your own thoughts.

Now, in terms of where you should begin your focus with the Sexy Boss process, this might shock you.

How to Transform Your Sexuality Into Higher Power

I'm convinced that sex – including sexual energy and passion -- is the most powerful force on earth. Being sexy connects us to our highest self because it's so tied into our creative power, both physically and energetically.

Napoleon Hill talks about that in *Think and Grow Rich* – observing that more sexual people are often more creative and more charismatic. They are successful at a higher level. They are able to go after what they want at a higher level with more grace and ease.

That's why – if you don't have a strong positive association with your own sexuality and sense of sexiness – you'll cripple yourself.

If you don't, that's okay. Take this as an opportunity to regain power over how you see yourself sexually. The only time you can ever do anything is right now. So get started.

For instance, maybe you're sexually frustrated. This happens to us all – whether we're in a relationship or not. And yet, how you see and relate to those feelings of frustration can make all the difference.

For instance, you can choose to look at the feelings of frustrated sexual energy and be negative and blame yourself or your partner. Or you can look and think, "Wow, look at all this energy! So much power in that energy, it's so beautiful."

And you can choose to feel that energy and channel it into a positive pursuit. See the difference?

It's the same if or when anyone has "made" you feel bad or inadequate sexually. If so, screw them. They were idiots. But it's over now, it can't be changed, and whether you choose to carry that around is your choice.

It's not that I don't feel compassion, I do. But compassion is not pity -- I don't pity people, I acknowledge and respect their power.

It's also important to understand the incredible sexual power and energy that exists between the two sexes, and how much we can affect one another.

Everything we've said about feelings, associations and what you focus on is amplified in the context of a sexual relationship. That's part of why relationships are such profound learning experiences -- because they can create so much pain (and growth) when you become aware of all this.

Of course, when you're able to maintain sexual high energy and creativity – through love, passion, support on that high level – you gain a tremendous amount of power. It's the difference between us and animals. They don't have that the ability to direct their sexual energy. They have, obviously, reproduction; but they don't have sexual energy in the way that we do.

How to Gain Unstoppable Personal Momentum And Power

And that brings me to the final point about being aware of your thoughts and associations, and consciously choosing power over victimhood.

The effect is cumulative. The more you do this, the happier and stronger you become, and you develop authentic power that attracts and inspires others.

That goes to the heart of how I define being a Sexy Boss, and why this is the second step in the process.

To conclude our discussion, let's take this process and make it as practical as possible.

Because this will only help you if you can successfully take action on what you discover.

So take a moment to think:
- Are there any negative patterns of thought that you notice recurring inside you? It could be surrounding money, sex, relationships, family, your abilities, or anything else…

- If so, and we all have them on some level, think about how you can potentially shift your focal point…

- Ask yourself, "What can be positive about this? How can it help me? Where can I go from here?" Notice how you may ignore or use excuses to avoid the issue.

- By learning to shift the way you look at something that might otherwise drag you down, *you'll gain energy and power.*

And ultimately, the best way to judge the effectiveness is simply to tune into how you feel.

Do you feel stronger? More empowered? More inspired about the possibilities that await you?

If so, great! If not, then keep at it.

Once you make the decision to move forward in this area, it will happen.

It's only a matter of time.

Final Thoughts from a Sexy Boss

The ability to shift your focus and concentrate on higher, more constructive thoughts is a skill – and one that won't happen overnight.

But the more you do it, the better you'll get. And you'll have taken the second step in realizing your full potential as a Sexy Boss.

Chapter 3

Killing Your Excuses and Stories

"Everybody's got a past. The past does not equal the future unless you live there." – Anthony Robbins

"The opposite of wealth attraction is wealth inhibition". – Dan Kennedy

Being a sexy boss is becoming a new person.

Part of that means be willing to kill your excuses and stories. It's about making the decision to stop letting them influence your life, and to let them die.

This purpose of this chapter is simple and two-fold:

1) To IDENTIFY the excuses, stories and limiting beliefs that come from your past... and...

2) Then STOP letting them be part of your life.

The Power of Tough Love

As women looking to win in a man's world is, we need more *tough love*. Many men have had plenty of tough love throughout their lives – from their fathers, their friends, or a coach who really cared enough to push them.

But from the time we were little girls, it was rare that we were ever pushed. And this is especially true if you were attractive. Most people (especially men) were too busy kissing your butt to ever truly level with you about the most important things.

We desperately need tough love. All of us – men AND women! We need that person who will flat out tell us, "Stop making excuses" or "you're selling yourself short" or "shut up and just do it".

Otherwise, it's possible to just wander through life with a false sense of reality – and never really get anywhere with our dreams and ambitions.

That's why in this chapter and throughout this Sexy Boss process I'm going to be giving you a lot of tough love. And I do it because I care about you. Because I know your potential and I know the ways we sell ourselves short and play small – because I've been guilty of them all at one point or another.

If you're the kind of person who can't handle a little honesty and tough love, then please put this book down. It's not for you.

Breaking Free from The Past Is Essential

A lot of people think breaking free from the past is only for those who have had a troubled past.

But in reality, breaking free from the past means letting go of positive and negative. You see, it's common to think we only need to forget about failures and the negative, but sometimes success – if it locks us into a limited way of doing things – can hold us back even more.

One example could be if you've always been very conservative financially. That can be a great thing! But then what if you need to take out a loan for a new business, or invest your savings in a new venture?

It may not be the most financially-wise decision by conventional or conservative thinking. But what if it's the best way to get your business started?

Remember, history is filled with cases of individuals making the ballsy decision to put everything into a business and making it big. So it could be that you'd miss the opportunity of a lifetime because you did what had "worked" or made you successful in the past.

Past Emotions That Hold Us Back

Another big part of the factor in freeing yourself from the past is *emotional* – especially guilt and fear. Left unexamined and lingering within, those emotions may create the most significant internal barrier to realizing your full sexiness and power.

For example, one of the most common forms of guilt might come as a surprise: the guilt of success.

Yes, this is totally real. Maybe you came from a neighborhood or community where success is not common, and as a result, you feel guilty about leaving those people behind. This type of emotional barrier can be especially common in families, where you feel guilty of succeeding if others in your family have not or all poor.

You could argue that this is one reason why many athletes actually end up going broke not long after their careers are over. They made it big, earned a lot of money, but also many had so family members and friends with no money – and felt guilty about their own personal success.

That sounds weird, but I was definitely one of the people that was afraid of success. In my experience, I became successful at a fairly young age. Partly due to the sense of fight and independence I mentioned in the last chapter. However, what I also experienced was that people attacked me, or came after my money (in the case of one of my business partners).

And that affected and shaped me. That initial experience was not about giving and loving, but about taking. They wanted to take something from me. So over a period of time

I played small because I felt guilt around the fact that I had the ability to be successful.

In a sense, I was playing small.

Go Big Or Go Home

I currently live in Austin, Texas – and in Texas, there's a popular phrase which says, "Go big or go home." I love it.

For me, it's really about always playing at our full capacity that we know that we can play at. For me, specifically, I knew that I had a lot to give. I knew that I could help more people. I knew that I could be a great sales person or a great contributor to society.

But I held myself back! No one was forcing me to do that. I was doing that.

And it took me seeing that – and getting really pissed off with myself, saying "enough is enough" and resolving to move forward.

Are you truly giving everything you can to what you want? You better believe it. We're all guilty of this. We all have this capacity for greatness that we often allow to lie dormant beneath the surface.

In my experience with myself and other people, it's common to hold ourselves back for fear or guilt of what others might think. That was mine.

"I don't want to become too successful," I subconsciously thought, "I'll just become a little bit successful, because if I'm really big then people will not like me. Or they'll attack me and come after me."

It was such BS, and it drove me crazy as I battled with it.

But it's all too common in this day and age. Remember, we all have an identity that's tied into those we know and have relationships with. Dramatic success threatens that identity because a radical change to it means people will be forced to see you differently.

This is why there was a part of me that strove to be "normal" – and why many people get caught in this pattern.

The problem is, when you don't push yourself and take risks – and you only play at the level that you know how to play, it limits you and keeps you small. You never expand beyond your baseline and never reach your true, full potential.

It's not being sexy, it's being a scared little pussy cat.

Stop Protecting a False Identity!

What's crazy is that we unconsciously think we are helping others by preserving our identity – that our success will somehow be a threat to them. What's even crazier is that the "small" identity we are protecting isn't even us!

I personally didn't help myself by playing beneath my potential, and I actually hurt myself. In reality, I was protecting a "false" version of me – a lesser version tied into the guilt and limitations of others.

God gave me gifts to be able to be the best that I can be, and I was denying everyone by selling myself short.

Can you imagine Oprah saying, "Oh, you know, I should just stop after year one or year two. I'm big enough. I need to stop now. I don't want the tabloids to write about me." It would have been terrible for everyone. She has contributed so much to the world.

Think of all the things she did and how many people's lives might not have changed had Oprah sold herself short. I mean she has changed millions of people lives, still is today even now with her own network.

Perhaps worst of all, when we unknowingly suppress our own potential, it's like putting a cork on our energy and magnetism. We become less attractive on a deeper, energetic level. People don't feel as drawn to us, or as inspired by us.

And this can become habitual. Not only becomes a habit, becomes a pattern that we are used to. As a Sexy Boss, you are essentially the CEO of your own life.

Thus, as a Sexy Boss it's crucial we say "no more!" to past failures, no more to past beliefs, no more past to excuses and inhibitions.

That's what I mean by not allowing fear to hold you down or stop you from doing what you know to do in your higher self. I believe that being a Sexy Boss is being connected to your higher self or to God or to your muse. Essentially, the source of your passion and inspiration.

Look Into The Mirror and Affirm Who You Really Are

Here's something fun you can do to help awaken the Sexy Boss within.

Pick a day (ideally when no one else is there to distract you) and then look in the mirror. Feel the most powerful, sexiest, most ambitious parts of yourself. Actually FEEL that energy coursing through your body and veins.

Next, look into your eyes and yell at the top of your lungs –
"I AM A SEXY BOSS!"

– with a big smile on your face. This is who you really are.

It's affirming your sexiness and the fact that you're in charge of your life and everything in it – from your health to your wealth, love and beyond.

Now, notice when you do say out loud, "I am a Sexy Boss!" Observe what you feel. Often, all the old beliefs, negative beliefs that come up with the word "sexy" and the words "being the boss".

These are all words that have old patterns attached to them for everyone's different. Being sexy might be something you're not allowed to be. Maybe ambition is sexy to you, so by denying your sexiness, you're sacrificing personal ambition. And the goals and dreams that go along with that.

How sad! The simple fact that you're reading this now tells me you want more for yourself than that.

You know damn well it's NOT okay to suppress or ignore your most ambitious dreams and desires. Deep down, you feel your extraordinary potential and sexiness – and you're ready to shine it out to the world.

That's why it's so crucial to be "reborn" so to speak. To allow the past – whoever you've been – to die. So that you can start fresh.

Now, I don't mean that you lose all your amazing memories or leave your family like a cult. Not at all.

As I've stated throughout, it's about freeing yourself from the beliefs and feelings that may currently be causing you to feel guilty or play small.

Where to Locate Limiting Beliefs and Feelings – The Usual Suspects

As you go through this process, one thing you'll discover about limiting beliefs and emotions is they tend to reside in certain places. Often the areas you care about most!

Let's look for a moment at the "usual suspects"

- Money
- Sex
- Sexiness (Being Sexy)
- Body image
- Health
- Success
- Career
- Self-esteem
- Dreams/aspirations
- Relationships
- Spirituality

This are all the most common areas where we might be held back by limiting beliefs or emotions.

And whether it's money, whether its health, whether it's looking your best, whether it's starting your own business, going after your dream job, you might already be held back and not realize it. So how do you get to that place where there is no fear around those areas?

Remember one of the quotes at the beginning of this chapter from Dan Kennedy: *"The opposite of wealth attraction is wealth inhibition".*

It can also be moved into other areas, because wealth inhibition is the same energy as being healthy, being fit, love inhibition, passionate inhibition.

So it's not that we can't be wealthy or whatever we want. It's that we actively (and often unconsciously) inhibit ourselves from that thing.

Stop Screwing Yourself Over

What if success and prosperity in every one of those areas we just covered – from health to relationships and beyond – could be totally natural and effortless?

In reality, I believe this to be true. Once you cut through all the BS, lies and half-truths – everything gets easier. Once we stop clouding our minds with stories and excuses, life isn't so hard.

Do you see where you hold yourself back? Do you justify why you're not living your full potential? That is a story, and one that doesn't serve you.

It could be that somebody told you that you weren't pretty long ago, so you spend years or decades thinking of yourself as not beautiful or not sexy.

But is that the truth? Really the truth? No effing way!

It's a false idea that was given to us from the outside, and for whatever reason, we've mentally or emotionally latched on to.

However, when you are freed up from the past, when you let go of what we're taught and you're able to know that wealthy or healthy or sexy or anything you want -- is unlimited. Everything is a choice and unlimited.

As The Boss and CEO of Your Life, You Get to Choose Everything

I've had many mentors along my journey and one of them is Mr. Richard Flint. He's a mentor and friend. He says, "To get beyond yesterday is to be able to create a new today. Don't let the yesterday be in your head today."

I was actually on the phone today with Richard and he told to me to do a powerful exercise.

He said, "Look in the mirror and say to yourself, to the old self, the old patterns, the old way of being, 'you are no longer in control of my life and your presence is no longer needed or requested. I, the new Heather Ann am in control of my life and I make new choices today.'"

Sexy Boss Exercise

Make a decision that you are ready to cross the line in your life. To leave the yesterday in yesterday. Next, as you are going along your day, in the car, looking in the mirror, wherever. Say out loud:

"I am the new 'your name' and I am in control of my life. Today I make new choices. Old 'nick name' you are no longer in control and your presence is no longer requested. Thank you for keeping me safe."

I found this exercise really powerful because one of the biggest challenges that we deal with is in relating to our old self.

I even have a name for mine. Mine is called "old weather Heather" because she brings bad weather to Heather. So I call her "old weather Heather".

For the new me is the new Heather Ann. And it's not that "old weather Heather" is bad, or the "old weather Heather" is not part of me.

It's just that her job is to keep me small. Her job is to hold me back. She wants to protect me, or so she thinks.

Unfortunately, if I let her run my life then she kills me off in all areas – my wealth, my health, my friendships, harmony relationships as well as relationships with my significant other. Many people live with a part of their psyche damaging or even totally sabotaging their dreams.

Which Wolf Are You Feeding?

There's an old Native American proverb that says:

A Native American boy was talking with his grandfather.

"What do you think about the world situation?" he asked.

The grandfather replied, "I feel like wolves are fighting in my heart.
One is full of anger and hatred; the other is full of love, forgiveness, and peace."

"Which one will win?" asked the boy.

To which the grandfather replied, "The one I feed."

Essentially, this is what we were just discussing – namely, that when you feed the negativity, it grows and gains power. Likewise with the other side of you.

So the question is – are you going to feed the negative part of you, the part that wants to play small and not take big risks that could hurt your ego?

Or are you going to feed the other side… the side of you that knows how sexy and passionate and amazing you are – and is willing to step into the spotlight and be great?

What side you feed makes all the difference in your life. Period.

Of course, it's not about abusing or judging a part of yourself as "bad". In fact, you can and should give love and acceptance to all parts of yourself – even the parts that appear to be sabotaging you.

However, what we're saying is to not give it power OVER you. Big difference. By being a Sexy Boss, you are making it be know that you're in charge now – you are running the ship.

And of course, you want to actively feed and nurture the parts of you that breed love, contribution, wealth, wealth mind set, harmony and relationship. More on how to do that as we progress through this book.

It Takes Real Courage to Move Forward

Keep in mind that something that happened to you in the past – especially if it was limiting or traumatic – may never be forgotten. And that's okay.

What's important is that you're able to go beyond that thing, not necessarily forget. Going beyond equates to moving forward, and doesn't require that you act like your past never happened.
Going beyond actually is truly about being free of something. Forgiving if you need to forgive yourself, forgiving the other person, grieving if there's something that needs to be grieved about. You get the point. It's about getting through it. Not over it. Not under it. Not around it.

Face your past – all of it – and go THROUGH it. That is real freedom.

It's also real courage, because it takes fearlessness and honesty to see when you avoid facing your past.

Part of how you'll know is when you catch yourself making excuses or telling stories as a way to justify something that's happening. You're late, so you say it was because of traffic... you have no money and it's because your parents didn't teach you how to manage money.

We covered all that in the first chapter, and you now know those excuses are simply not real.

To get beyond the past, you have to acknowledge that you're responsible right now. That you are creating every moment – in the present. Only when you do that will you have the clarity and the freedom to live today. To be everything you want to be as a Sexy Boss!

Part of how you do this is by drawing a line in the sand.

Internally, it's about saying, "No more. No more am I going to feel guilty for success. No more am I going to feel fear for going after what I want in life. No more am I going to give myself excuses that it is not the right time. No more am I going to hold myself back in inhibition that this is not the right thing for me to do."

Letting go of the yesterday creates the ability to have forward thinking, forward thoughts, going after what you want, no holding back. It's never going to go away. Fear will always be there. It's moving beyond it and past it.

I believe it's a choice. *I know it's a choice.* Being able to be a Sexy Boss of your own life and being the CEO of your own life is being aware and in command of all parts of yourself, through some of the insights and communications we've been discussing.

How I Broke Free of The Past

For me, as we learned earlier, my guilt has been in being successful. I thought, "If I'm successful, someone will take the money from me." That comes from something that happened to me when I was around eight.

When I was a little girl, I had this dream that I was going to be able to save enough money to get a car for myself at 16.

With that dream in mind, I did chores around the house and got an allowance which I saved. I also did all sorts of little things, like a lemonade stand for example, in order to make a buck wherever I could.

I saved and then saved some more. I kept every single penny in this orange and black polka-dot shoebox. That was my secret, and I stored the box right underneath my bed. Sometimes at the end of school day I'd run up the stairs, pull it out, and and count how much money I had. Then I'd go ask my mom, *"How much money is a car?"*

She'd say $5,000 or $10,000 or whatever cars cost back then -- and then I would say, "Oh God. If I could save this amount of money each year between now and I'm 16, I think I can do it!" I would use little calculations and I was really trying hard.

Then One Day It Happened

One afternoon, and I still remember how I felt to this day, I went upstairs and I went underneath the bed to check on my money. I pulled out my secret shoebox and opened it. To my horror, it was empty. TOTALLY EMPTY. All gone.

I start to tear up and cry. My mom walked in and I said, "My money is gone. My money is gone!" She had this look in her eye and she says, "Oh my God, the maids must have took it." The maids came in that day and had cleaned the house, so there was no way to prove otherwise.

However, I kind of knew in the back of my head that my Mom had taken it. She was the only one who really knew about it. I never asked her about that, but I think a part of me unconsciously felt, "I better not be successful. People will take my money."

So growing up, I went through that experience and held onto that belief. I didn't really deal with it much. I even kind of forgot about it. So I'm going through life and I'm becoming really successful in my career, but I tried to make it invisible. Meaning I didn't really show it or tell people I was successful.

You can probably see how this relates to the story I told you in the last chapter. About how, back in 2005, I started a business with two gentlemen.

As you now know, we were doing over million dollars in sales within six months of launching -- which is insane for a startup business. Many companies take years to get to that level, and we were doing that in the first year. Crazier yet, I was the CEO and running it. My first real business of my own, and we were exploding.

Then, as you learned last chapter, one day I went to a seminar for three days in Atlanta, drove back to Orlando and discovered that everything was gone.

The people, the equipment, all the money -- GONE.

Just Like My Shoebox!

Again history repeats itself. I am successful, working my butt off and someone takes it all away.

Understandably, it took me a long time to move through the pain of that pattern and be able to say, *"What was that all about?"* I was guilty. I felt guilty for being successful. I felt that I wasn't allowed to be successful because if I did, someone would just take it away.

I had to re-frame that experience in order to move forward. I had to use the lesson to further my own personal commitment to be a Sexy Boss, and master of my own destiny. I had to let go of the fear people would take my success away from me.

That meant no more guilt, no more fear. Going after what I want, being clear on what I want, being wisely protective but not avoiding worthwhile risks because of what had been taken from me in the past.

Slowly, I began to trust again.

More importantly, I allowed myself to be bold and courageous, to take risks knowing that even though I could fail, the only to win is to get back in the game and play at 100%.

When you do that, the potential reward is always infinitely greater than the risk.

How to Be Totally Real With Yourself

Obviously, I know letting traumatic events like this go are not easy! It's not about saying, *"Oh well, that happened,"* and forgetting it. I had to go through several crucial steps:

The first was getting real, being real about what happened and what didn't happen all the way back from when I was eight years old.

The second step was to forgive myself. Not blaming or hating myself for what happened. Acknowledging that I learned a lot in those business situations, and also forgiving myself that it happened.

The third step is to forgive the other person. It's normal to get really mad at mom or get really angry at those other people. Believe me I did and I tried to go after them.

However, I looked at should I really attack them now? It's been six years. Do I just focus on being my best, empowering myself as a Sexy Boss and knowing the "living well is the best revenge"?

Yes, I believe that's what we should do for anyone who has wronged you.

The best revenge is "Live Your Best Life, Today!"

So it was tough, but I had to forgive them and let that go. (I'm not saying legal action is never appropriate, it's important to stand up for yourself when the time comes. Just that in my case, it would have cost me much more than it would have given me.)

And there was no way I was going to let that story run my life. No effing way.

Then from there I had to create a new pattern. I couldn't just do it again. I had to create a new pattern for myself.
For me, that new pattern is what I call being the Sexy Boss, being able to know that I can do it with a great team. I could do it for myself and for others. I can really be at my best and shine, and that's best gift I can give myself.

Again, It's All About Personal *Responsibility*

All this comes back to taking personal responsibility on many different levels.

In order to forgive some body you have to be responsible for that.

Responsibility is power and moves you away from being victim. I could easily have become the victim in both the situations. In many cases in my head, many hours I spent there, but it didn't serve me. It wasn't powerful for me. It wasn't a powerful place for me to come from. I wasn't being a boss of myself or my life.

Also being revengeful and angry is not something that's being responsible as a leader of my life.

I think of really big successful people, Donald Trump, Oprah Winfrey, many others -- these people are 100% responsible for everything that happens in their life and everything that doesn't happen in their life.

They're not victims or martyrs or say, *"Look, they did that to me. Oh, People Magazine said this about me."*

In a positive sense, they have blinders on. Meaning they focus on what they need to focus on and they're 100% responsible for everything they have and everything they don't.

In that sense, responsibility equals power. At that level, you have no one else to blame if something goes wrong, because you're in charge.

No excuses, no stories about why you can't do something. Just commitment and courage in action.

You have that in you now, stop pretending like you don't.

Final Thoughts from a Sexy Boss

This chapter is largely about laying the groundwork for success. To use a farming metaphor, it's tending to the soil – so that the seeds you plant later in this process can take root and grow abundantly.

By looking within and freeing yourself of past limitations and patterns, you prepare yourself for radically new possibilities.

Remember, being a Sexy Boss means taking the very best of you – and becoming a new person.

Because as soon as you stop making excuses for yourself, your past does not equal your future, and you can create anything you want. Starting today.

Chapter 4

The Real Definition of Sexy

"People think that if you're sexy you have no brains, and if you have brains you aren't in touch with your sexual side. I'm trying to tell people, 'You can have it both ways." – Erica Durance (Canadian Actress and Producer)

What does it _really_ mean to be sexy?

Does that mean you have to have tan, toned body like Jennifer Aniston -- or a stunningly beautiful face like Catherine Zeta Jones?

The answer is NO. Of course, Jennifer Aniston and Catherine Zeta-Jones and many wonderful actresses are beautiful, sleek and sexy. That's not what I mean by being sexy.

Being a Sexy Boss is really about confidence on every level.

It's a true self-expression of who you are deep down, as a powerful creative woman who makes things happen.

Does that mean that being "sexy" is accepted in today's business culture?

Unfortunately, no. Many of those in business -- men and women -- are even more threatened by a woman's power than they are by her physical sexiness.

That's why it's so important to affirm your sexiness, and ideally, create your own business where it doesn't matter what others within the corporate structure think of you. More on that later in this book.

For now, just realize that being sexy is more than just being "hot" or "beautiful" -- it's reconnecting with the most powerful, most charismatic parts of you. And then bringing them into everything you do.

THAT is Sexy Boss.

Does Being Sexy Make You a "Slut"?

Absolutely not!

In today's society, even though things are more liberal, we are still unfortunately bound to many of our past limiting perceptions about women and sexiness.

Remember, being sexy and being a Sexy Boss is NOT about openly flaunting your sexuality, wearing skimpy clothes, or any of that.

It is, however, definitely about owning and being confident as a sexual, human being.

If you're powerful or beautiful or you have high sexual energy, you've perhaps had negative experiences where you've been labeled or treated inappropriately.

Part of the Sexy Boss movement and pledge is helping to reverse that tendency, by helping those in the business world see what it really means to be sexy -- and why it's so valuable. Especially in business!

That's why it's so important that you go through this process and affirm everything you learn here. Because we need more women who stand up to the status quo and notion that being sexy and powerful makes you a threat.

Again, it's not about dressing sexually or flirting -- it's about who you are.

Think about it like this:

Have you ever had an experience of meeting a person you're just attracted to... someone you're just magnetically attracted to? You might not even know who they are or anything about them, but you're just automatically attracted to who they are.

This Has *Nothing* to Do With Looks!

They may or may not be extremely good looking. They are just very attractive.

One example of a man who is not stereotypically handsome or great looking is Bill Clinton, especially now that he's older. Yet Bill Clinton has extremely high level charisma (he also has high levels of sexual energy).

And yet, it's his charisma that helped him get elected as the President of the United States of America. In fact, when he recently spoke at the Democratic National Convention, people were so amazed and awe-struck -- you'd think Clinton could easily be elected now!

His charisma (which I believe is closely tied to his sexual energy) is what attracted so many voters and people sometimes don't even know why. They would just say things like, "I just love that Bill Clinton." Even Newt Gingrich, one of his sworn enemies, used to have to walk out of meetings with Clinton and remind himself how much he hated him. Because Clinton was just so charming and charismatic.

On the female side, there are many examples of this -- some beautiful and others not so conventionally beautiful. One is Sophia Vergara, a star of the hit show Modern Family. She started out as a model and Spanish TV actress, then came here and took a long time before she really made it.

But I bring her up because even though she's beautiful -- Sophia has a sensual quality and elegance about her that makes her sexy. What's more, she's very passionate about what she does, she knows what she wants, and she's made so much happen at a time when most actresses would have given up. That is being Sexy Boss.

Some other inspiring examples might be Oprah. Pretty much everyone knows about Oprah, but few know just how much she's battled with her weight, her relationships, how much adversity she's been through to become the billionaire Sexy Boss that she is.

Another great one would be Roseanne Bar -- the comedian. Yes, on the surface she has always been overweight and perhaps not the prettiest woman in the world -- but who cares. Roseanne was a badass comedian, who helped created one of the most successful TV shows ever. It ran for many years, led the ratings, won Emmy's. She could have said, "I'm overweight" or "I'm not beautiful enough" and quit -- but she believed in what she could do and didn't apologize or make excuses. She just did it. That's sexy!

And that's the kind of sexy power I want you to gain by reading this book.

How I Suppressed My Own Sexiness

The reason why I'm so passionate about the word "sexy" in Sexy Boss is partly due to my own experience. Ever since I was 17 or 18, I've always been looked at as "sexy" physically, but that it was not a good thing. And by default, all the other sexy qualities I had inside of me were bad too.

So I always had to cover up myself. If ever I was in business environment, I would wear really large suits that were two times my size. The jacket would go past my hips and I wore baggy pants. I thought I had to dress like a guy in business. I didn't really own my sexuality as a woman. I was not very confident in that situation. I was always trying to cover up my femininity. So when I was working for Corporate America back in 2000, I was working in a situation where it was all males. I was wearing these big suits. I was wearing turtlenecks. I was wearing all pants. I was wearing flat shoes.

I mean if you know me now, you would laugh because that's just not who I am. But I thought that's what I was supposed to do. Even in that situation, my energy was still sexual, but I was very not confident.

I was so clearly holding myself back, which is never sexy. It doesn't mean I should have been wearing short skirts all the time -- just that I was ashamed of my sexiness and covered myself up.

How to Be Sexy In The Workplace Without It Backfiring

I remember at one of my first corporate jobs, there was an older gentleman who expressed interest in working more closely with me. It was flattering and I didn't realize what he wanted.

I was kind of naïve about it. I just thought he was being nice and I thought he was just being a mentor. And as you might guess, the reality is he wanted to get me in bed.

So when we got to that point and I said "no" he was shocked. Now, I can see how he thought I was perhaps leading him on. In my mind, I was not at all, but at the same time I do have a lot of sexual energy and as much as I tried to suppress it, I could not.

So as I told him, "No, I'm not interested." And then few weeks later I got moved to another team, and then few weeks after that, I got let go from the company. I picked up the phone and called an attorney and had the conversation.

Here's what happened. She said to me, "Look, you do have a case. You have a case and there is something legitimate here. However, I need you to understand how our society works today. If you go through this and if you win let's say a million dollars, this is how this is going to be played out."

She continued, "Your name and face is going to be placed across every single form of media, and you'll be portrayed in many ugly ways -- from slut, to gold digger, to seductress and beyond. They're going to try to kill your reputation as much as possible before they ever get to trial -- if we ever get that far."

Ultimately, she said she would support my decision either way, but she just wanted me to be aware of the consequences. So I thought, "Okay, what can I learn from this? What can I learn from this situation?" I made a conscious decision not to go after that person.

Of course, as Karma has it, about a year later he got fired actually from the same company because of a sexual harassment.

So it's karma, but I learned something there and I learned that it was not about him. He did something wrong because I was a beautiful young woman. However, I didn't own my sexuality. Had I been stronger in regard to my own sexuality, I could have read his intentions better and also established more firm boundaries.

I just know that if that same thing had happened to me now, the first time he flirted or made an inappropriate comment I would have firmly told him, *"Look, you're a man, I get that. But that is not appropriate. I'm a professional and if you're not going to treat me as such, then I suggest we do not communicate."*

Since I've learned how to be sexy AND still have strong boundaries, I've never had a situation where I felt that I was taken advantage of ever again.

How Do You USE Your Sexual Energy to Be More Successful?

This is an important question. I remember a while back a boyfriend told me, "Heather, you could be sexy if you're wearing a burlap sack." When I first heard that I thought, "Oh, my God, what's wrong with me? What does he mean by I could be sexy in a burlap sack? That's crazy. I can't be sexy in a burlap sack. I need to have my high heels on."

To me, sexy was being in high heels and a short skirt. That's what it looked like for me then, but now I understand now that sexual energy is creative energy. And ultimately, that it can be used in any situation for greater creativity.

When I was closed down sexually, those years that I had those big large jackets, big baggy pants on, you couldn't tell if I even had a body much less boobs at all -- I wore those clothes because I was closed off creatively. I wasn't allowing myself to be free and express my creative faculty. What I mean by creative faculty is our own creative energy and manifestation.

I believe that when we are creative, we are expressing ourselves on a deep and passionate level. And in those moments, we are manifesting or creating our own reality on a higher level and a faster pace. So let me explain.

Reasoning and knowledge function in our heads. That is useful. However, if you get too much in your head or too focused on what you think you know, that is NOT creative energy.

It is in nature a faculty that's based on one's past. Therefore, it's limited. Sexual or creative energy is more reliable I feel because it's felt in the present, from a more authentic place, and it's limitless.

So when one is being what I call a Sexy Boss, they are owning who they truly are, their authentic self. They're owning the fact that, at their core, they are a sexual human being.

Be Sexy and Grow Rich

Napoleon Hill, author of the best-selling classic, *Think and Grow Rich,* calls this process *"Sex Transmutation."* It's one of the most controversial and misunderstood, yet also vitally-important parts of his work.

He says:

Number one: Those who have realized the greatest achievements tend to be men with highly developed sex natures. These men have learned the art of sex transmutation, which is about channeling sexual energy into a higher-level pursuit.

Number two: The men who have accumulated great fortunes and achieved outstanding recognition in literature, art, industry, architecture or other professions were motivated by the influence of a woman.

This "inspiration" helped them tap into their sexual energy, which then got transmuted into something higher and more creative.

It Sounds Very "Woo Woo"
But In Reality, It's Biological

Look, I know this might sound like a bunch of New Age mumbo jumbo.
However, just think about animals for a moment. When you neuter a dog or cat, they become more docile, less active. You castrate a bull and it becomes as docile as a cow.

You literally lose a huge source of the energy that drives your body and other parts of you. The two highest vibrations that we as human beings can create is one is the desire for sexual expression. Number two is love and number three is the desire for power and or financial gain.

There's all kinds of stories about most murderers or tragedies are based on rage of sex and money. You've heard that most marriages end because of either, sex or money. Well, that's because they're tied into the top three emotions of human beings.

I think many religious institutions don't want to talk about sex or money because they say it's evil. It's also the opposite. The desire for sex and money have fueled some of the greatest efforts and achievements in the history of mankind.

Your job right now as a Sexy Boss is to get more in touch with your urges and energy around the topics of sex, money and power -- and then be sure you're not suppressing or judging yourself for anything.

Once you've cleared that, you'll be ready to start focusing those desires and energy in the direction of more positive, more elevated pursuits.

How I Learned to Direct My Sexual Energy And Use It To Fuel Success

I came from a sales background in corporate America. Even before that I used to work in the financial services industry and I'll get to that in a minute. In many situations, it was not the product or me that sold the customer. It was my personal charisma or personal magnetism, in that moment.

However, in my younger years in corporate America I didn't really know what was driving that. I just felt like I had a good day or a bad day. I had no way to consistently bring that forth and have that consistently happen.

I thought it was because of random things, like what I drove or what I wore or whether the product that was good or bad. Or how I showed it or what I said. So I went to all these different sales training seminars, which focused on how to say the right thing, or do the right thing to "close the deal." Soon, I became number ONE out of 10,000 other reps of the entire country in a large company. Being young, if you had told me the day that I learned I was number one. You say, "How did you do it?" I would look at you and say, "I have no idea," because I was just driving so hard that I had no idea why I was successful or if I had to repeat it, I didn't know how to do it.

I did not truly understand why one day I would make massive, massive sales. The next day I didn't.

Now, what's interesting is few years prior, I worked for American Express Financial Advisers. They have now turned into a new company. I was an assistant. I got to work for many different financial advisers during my college years. I made phone calls for them and did all kinds of things, including basic tasks like copying and filing documents.

I found it interesting that the men who were most successful often knew the least about the finance side of business. They really knew very little about stocks and what's really happening on Wall Street. They actually knew the least, but they were the most financially successful on the business side. I could never understand why until I made the connection between charisma and success.

Sexual Energy = Charisma

When you stop suppressing and start freeing up your sexual energy, you instantly become more charismatic.

But how does this energy and charisma get communicated to others? How do others know that you have this energy?

I believe there are at least five different ways that "it" gets communicated.

1) The handshake. I'm sure there's a been a time where you've met an extremely attractive man or woman, and you've shook their hand. Their hand is limp. Feels like nothing, no energy. Or the opposite, you shake their hand and it feels like they're trying so hard to be strong, as if to crush you. There's a lot you can feel in one's handshake.

2) The tone of their voice. This includes how they speak and the overall energy of it. It doesn't even matter what they say. It's the tone of the voice. It's the feeling you're getting when you hear their voice.

I always think of Barbara Walters or Larry King because they were such great communicators. People loved opening up to them and felt amazing trust. If you just look at them and who they are, they had high charismatic energy overall.

3) Their posture. How someone presents themselves is literally contained within their body posture. Seeing somebody with the slumped shoulders or they are looking away from you shows weakness or insecurity. Likewise, if they're biting their fingernails. All these are different ways of body alignment and posture.

4) Vibration of thought. This is a very powerful one, one that I got reminded of this morning. The vibration of thought is extremely powerful. For me, there's been an old saying. People told me, "Heather, you could kill a room or you can make a room as bright as the sun, all by your thought."

We get to choose our thoughts. We get to choose how that energy is projected. So if you walk into a room, walk into a situation in business, you walk into your office, walk into your home and you just look at your kids or you look at your husband with those glaring eyes or just think about something negative -- it will be felt.

There's vibration that's put out there even if you don't say a word. We've all experienced that and that is how energy gets communicated to others. It's extremely important as Sexy Boss to be aware of our thoughts and the energy they cause us to send out into the world.

5) Body adornment. I don't just mean your physical body, but the overall image and impression you create physically -- from your hair and clothes, to anything that is part of your physical adornment.

Think about someone like Catherine Zeta Jones. She could be a sexy boss and she's wearing an old white t-shirt and jeans and flip flops, not just because she's beautiful, but also because of who she's being and her energy gets communicated. She's a Sexy Boss.

It helps that she takes care of herself, from her complexion, the fitness of her body, her hair and so on. The point is that she takes care of herself on the outside as well as the inside.

The Beauty of Body Adornment

It's important to adorn your body in ways that represent who you are. The word "adorn" literally means to make more beautiful or attractive. This doesn't mean that you should try to fit into the styles or ideals created by others -- the opposite in fact.

That's something I personally discovered after years of traveling around the country -- I learned to adore my body, to allow myself to wear things that I found comfortable, that I enjoyed myself in.

One of the things I started to do when I lived in Florida is wear lots of colors. I don't know why, but I grew up in Texas and everything was brown. As soon as I moved to Florida I noticed everyone was wearing colors. Men, women, everyone wore colors. Men would wear really loud Tommy Bahama shirts and then khaki pants and flip flops. I never saw that before.

They wear really loud golf shirts, loud colors. I just found myself happier when I was wearing colors.

And so I did it. It was as simple as that. I didn't worry about what others would think, or hold myself back.

This is important because we're always presenting and selling ourselves. What others think shouldn't matter to our self-esteems or identity, but it does matter in terms of getting what we want as a Sexy Boss.

So it's important that you find what works for you, makes you feel confident and sexy -- AND at the same time also helps you get what you want.

Now I realize that if you're a woman reading this -- especially if you're born before 1950 in American culture -- you probably heard things like, *"Are you really going to wear that? You look slutty,"* or something like that. *"Are you really going to wear that outside?"*

This is common, and maybe you've got into the habit of suppressing your natural desires in the area of clothing or style. However, I urge you to use this process to make a shift.

Express yourself! Forget what other people think. Women, who are clearly wearing what they love and free with their personal style, are always sexier. And that's true whether they are 30 or 70.

I can't tell you what to wear, but I can tell you to NEVER wear anything that doesn't make you feel sexy, free and powerful.

Don't Hate People Because They're Beautiful

I remember when I heard Kathy Ireland speak in person one time. She's so beautiful. She's just stunning. I saw her speak and I personally was awed by her beauty not only in the outside, but the inside. When she spoke she was just amazing.

She talked about after she was a supermodel, after she did the cover of Sports Illustrated, all the massive success she had. She was successful in the world of modeling, and people looked at her as only that.

She was just a model. She wasn't taken seriously. It took her almost 15 years to overcome that through building a massively successful business. She talks about one of her biggest assets was her beauty at first, but one of her biggest negatives during business was her beauty because she had to overcome so much for people to take her seriously.

Then in 2012, she made the cover of Fortune Magazine. So if I ever get a chance, I would absolutely love to interview her. To me, she is a Sexy Boss because she overcame what others said about her and then used that to drive her forward.

Remember: Many people have their own personal inferiority complexes. But you have to learn to ignore them.

Even though people like to look at magazines and beautiful people, I can't tell you how many times especially women are like this and men too.

I remember I had a situation that I was applying for. I was applying for this position and I was perfect for the job. There was a gentleman who was interviewing me, and the position was that I'd be working with him directly.

He liked me. Then we met and he said, "I can't hire you." I said, "Why?"

"Because I won't be able to deal with my wife, she would be jealous of you and I don't want to deal with that." And he said this even though I was the perfect person for the job, and we got along great. I had great credentials. I was attractive and that was a problem. So both sexes are guilty of this.

The worst part of all of this is that when you express negativity toward others you feel are attractive, or you belittle them, *you actually make yourself less attractive!* Or as in the case of Kathy Ireland, when you underestimate them because they are beautiful, you cut yourself off from opportunities.

Just imagine the investors who passed on Kathy Ireland who are now kicking themselves after seeing how lucrative her businesses have become.

Going Beyond Just Sex

The sexier you become, the more people will try to put you in a box. Even if your sexiness is primarily non-physical and you're really powerful, people will still try to discredit you or underestimate other parts of what you can offer.

Like Kathy Ireland, she knew she had more to give, but in many situations women become so trained to feel that's all they have. Of course, it's not true. But if you're told something long enough, or something is communicated to you for most of your life, you tend to believe it.

Men do this too. I've met amazing men who feel the need to be with many sexual partners -- just to validate themselves, even when they're in a committed relationship. They can't stop because it's feeding the source of their insecurity.

Sexual addiction or overemphasis is a very serious thing. It can be the demise of a great human being. We saw that with Tiger Woods. We saw that Bill Clinton. Remember what we said about learning to transmute that sexual energy into something higher, it's so crucial.

Sometimes, in the case of men like Tiger or Bill Clinton, their energy was so intense and abundant, it's almost like it spun out of control. And it caused them great losses. Tiger lost an amazing woman, his wife. I do not fault these men for being attracted to other women. Part of that is a biological urge that is not always easy to control. However, I believe that the management of this energy is key to making smart decisions -- rather than mistakes.

As a woman, this is especially important because you won't get the second chance that many men make when they make big mistakes. You'll be branded in harsher ways, so it's imperative that while you free your sexual/creative energy -- that you also learn to direct it and establish proper boundaries.

We'll cover that more in later chapters and throughout the Sexy Boss process.

Leveraging Sexual Energy to Take You Higher

The emotions of love, sex and romance are timeless -- they are a huge part of what it means to be a human being. And often, they're the driving motivation for us through life.

They're also often the reason behind the pursuit of money.

Because, in reality, I believe there are many different levels of being rich. Rich does not just mean financial independence.

Being rich can just mean engaging in a labor of love, having fulfilled life or achieving something that's very personally meaningful to you.

Freedom from fear, also, is a way of being rich.
All these forms of wealth can be a driving factor in the pursuit of sex. We seek out a beautiful partner, in part, because of how they make us feel about ourselves. We seek out love because of the sense of intimacy and belonging it provides.

That is all beautiful to me. We want romance, love, connection... even wealth... and so much more -- all driven in part by the sexual energy that we have inside us. That's a wonderful thing. Don't be ashamed of that! Instead, actively leverage it to further fuel the pursuit of what you want, and the design of your sexy boss life.

This is what it means to be a Sexy Boss -- it's about owning who you are as a sexual human being. Man or woman, heterosexual, homosexual, it's about allowing that sexual energy to be released into the world in the form of drive, creativity, motivation and power.

It's power for you in business. It's power for you in money. It's power for you in the world of sex and love and even spirituality. Everything!

So don't be ashamed of your sexiness or your power --
instead, LEVERAGE IT to get everything you've ever
dreamed of.

That's what exactly I'm showing you how to do, here in this
book and anywhere that I communicate with you.

Final Thoughts from a Sexy Boss

The real definition of sexy is taking 100% responsibility for
wherever you're at in your life, and making the clear,
confident decision to move forward. No excuses, no
exceptions. Just do it.

Being a Sexy Boss is tapping into the limitless power that
lies in your sexuality, and then using that energy to drive
your life to greater and greater heights.

Chapter 5

Finding Your "Fire" As a Woman

"The starting point of all achievement is desire. Keep this constantly in mind. Weak desires bring weak results, just as a small amount of fire makes a small amount of heat." – Napoleon Hill

We've already done a lot of groundwork.

By now, you've got a sense of the mindset you'll need to push forward as a Sexy Boss woman. In this chapter, we're covering red hot desire and how you can find this "fire" within you as a business and a truly successful woman.

This is essential for you not only getting started as a Sexy Boss, but also persisting through the challenges that you'll face -- both internal and external.

Once you learn how to tap into this fire on a consistent basis, there's no limit to what you can do, both in business and personally.

How I Found My Fire at an Early Age

It was 1997, I was at Texas Christian University which is a university in Fort Worth, Texas, living in the dorms and being what I call a typical college student.

I was working as a hostess at night in the weekends at a nice restaurant in town. And one day, the week of finals, I got a call from my father and he says to me, *"Hey, I got your tuition bill, and we don't have the money to pay to it. We won't be paying anymore of your bills. Good luck."*

I was devastated. This was the end of finals week, and I didn't have time to get financial aid. It was over. Now I had this big bill, and if I didn't pay the bill, I couldn't come back to school.
So I was devastated. I finished my finals and then immediately moved in with my friends off campus in a place that resembled the MTV show, *The Real World.*

The rug of my life I felt was pulled away, and it was fast. I was scared and full of fear. And people told me I should just give up, go get a job and drop out of college. Because there was no way was I going to be a hostess and pay this very large bill from a private university.

But the one thing in my life I promised myself is that I would get a degree no matter what. I had a red hot desire, a commitment and passion to complete my education no matter what the circumstances.

So six months later, I found myself at a job interview at the ripe age of 20 for an executive sales position. Yes, an executive sales person at just 20 years old! I told you I was on fire, didn't I?

It was a fairly large Fortune 1,000 Company in the Dallas, Fort Worth area. Most of the sales executives and professionals were in their 30s and 40s. And so I sat there in front of this manager and said, "Look, I know I'd be great at sales."

I never had "sales experience" before. And so hemmed and hawed, resisting and trying to talk me out of it. He tried his best to give me a customer service position, but I wouldn't budge.

He treated me like I was a cute little girl. With my energy, sweet personality and big smile, I'd be a really great customer service rep for them inside their store. I said, "No, no, it wouldn't pay the bills for me, and it's not the job that I came here for."

"I WANT THE EXECUTIVE SALES JOB."

I made my intentions crystal clear. He kept insisting and I kept saying, "No."

Finally, after a few hours in his office, he said, *"Okay, I'll give it a try. I'll try to convince my superior manager, see if she'll allow it."*

Now, what's interesting about her superior manager, she was a woman. And when I walk into her office a few weeks later I told her the same story and I was determined. She could tell I was determined. "All right, go ahead," she said. And I did.

So I started in the outside sales position which, by the way, was the highest turnover position at the store. It was the highest paid because it was a commission, but it was also the highest turnover. In those situations, you don't want even to talk to your neighbor at the desk next to you because they'll be gone in three months.

With that burning hot desire, I had killed off any other possibilities. I didn't look anywhere else. I was determined to get that job and use it to pay my tuition.

I was like like a horse finishing a race in the Kentucky Derby. I knew I could use it to make my money and then finish my degree at night. And what drove me was not the money at the job. What drove me at that job was getting my degree.

And not long after, I was walking across my graduation stage with my diploma in hand. And then around that same time, I walked across the stage to receive my "Inner Circle Award" because I was one of the top ten out of 10,000 reps across the country in sales that year.

So I did it. I did not only finish college while having a great job and making money, I also paid for my tuition.

And because it was a Fortune 500 company, they helped to pay for my tuition at the same time. That was a huge stepping stone in my life. A situation where the rug was pulled out from underneath me. It really looked like there was no way I was going to be able to finish my degree, and yet through the power of red hot desire, I did it.

Focus on Enthusiasm and Passion, Not Excitement

Excitement is fleeting. It is something that goes and comes and goes. It's connected in a very weak way to your deeper motivations.
I see excitement like being on a rollercoaster. You get on and it's like "Whoa!" "Yeah!" and then it's over. That was exciting. And about 15 minutes later when something else comes across your path, that new thing becomes exciting.

It reminds me of like a six-year-old, where everything is exciting to them but whatever you put in front of them is exciting to them, right? It's just excitement for no other reason other than just excitement.

Enthusiasm is different. Enthusiasm is something internal. It's an internal desire and energy that surpasses excitement. Enthusiasm is what drives you in the midst of pain or upset or discouragement beyond what you think is possible.

Enthusiasm is usually connected to something deeper and more intrinsic to you as a person. If you're enthusiastic about politics, that usually stays with you. Or marketing. Or business. Or sports. It doesn't come and go like excitement does.

This Is Something Every World Class Athlete Has

The best athletes in the world, the ones that achieve the most, don't focus on excitement. Sure, they may get a little excited about a big event. But fundamentally they are enthusiastic and passionate about their sport. That's why they are so consistently drive.

They show up and give 100% for their team, for their own confidence, for their goals. They couldn't go through all those practices, all the blood, sweat and tears, if all they had was just excitement.

They're excited to be at the Olympics, but the excitement is not going to get them to that goal, to that finish line. It's the enthusiasm, passion and red hot desire within who they are that's going to get them to that last stroke, that last turn on the track.

In the world of motivational speaking and personal development, many of the old school seminars were very exciting. You leave the event on a high but this wouldn't translate into action or results after the event.

It was just excitement and nothing more.

Being a Sexy Boss Is a Marathon NOT a Sprint

While you need to move fast as a Sexy Boss, it's really a marathon. Because you'll need to go the extra mile and endure a variety of challenges, inner and outer. This is not to scare you, it's just reality.

Take Bikram Yoga as an example. It's a 90 minutes of Yoga where you're in a room listening to the instructor for 90 minutes in a 105-degree heat room. One by one, you're moving through 26 different positions.

It's probably one of the hardest things I put myself through. And every year they have an event called the 60-day challenge where you actually do 60 classes in 60 days straight.

And the class is a full hour and a half, no exceptions. When you think about time to get there and get changed and everything, you're looking at about a two and a half hours of every day.

And that's grueling. It's very dehydrating, and it's hard on your body. It's also fantastic for your body, it's extremely beneficial, but it's mentally and physically challenging.

And I've done the 60-day challenges now two years in a row. The first week I'm excited, but that second week, third week and beyond, the excitement is gone. I am not excited about going to that sweat room. But it's really about the burning desire and the decision that I made, and enthusiasm for what I'm going to get at the end of the process. THAT is what keeps me going to that hot room day after day.

> Quote: *"There's nothing better than being yourself." ~ Christina Fernandez De Kirchner (First elected female President of*

6 Steps To Turning Your Burning Desire Into Reality

Now let's uncover the six steps needed to turn your desires into reality and attract what you want in *any* area of your life.

Let's pretend that you want to earn more money, as soon as possible.

Step 1: Define what you want. In the case of money, it's about fixing in your mind the exact amount of money you desire. The words "I want plenty of money" is not definite, or "I want to be rich" is not specific enough. So fix your mind the exact amount of money you desire and write that down. So it could be to make $200,000 in the next six months.

Step 2: Determine exactly what you intend to give. Yes, you will need to give something in order to get the money you desire. Money is energy, and money is an exchange. For example, comedian Jim Carey wrote a future check out for himself in the amount of $10 million, for services rendered of acting.

He actually wrote it on the physical check, services rendered of 'acting'. It happened.

He actually cashed the check for $10 million.

At the time he wrote it he was broke, and that experience or that possibility of having a contract that large was nowhere in sight. However, his burning desire and commitment made it reality.

Your exchange could be totally different. Maybe it's running that business you've always wanted. Or working in the career that makes your heart sing. It could being an expert and selling your products online.

Whatever it is, the most important thing is that you're willing to exchange something meaningful in return for what you want.

Many people talk about how they want money to buy something. It could be a car. It could be medical bills, it could be anything. They need to help their family with medical bills, something is going on. It's a serious issue. They need money for that. But in the world of money, there's always an exchange. Always!

And the critical piece is focusing on what are you going to give in return for that money. Next is...

Step 3: Establish a date. This is when you intend to possess the money you desire. There needs to be a specific timeline, like it's going to be December 2015 by 1:00 p.m. Get really specific.

The reason why the specificity of time is so important is that it acts like "focus system". By doing that, you are actually putting the goal in a time and space reality. It's out of the ephemeral world and one step closer to reality.

It also focuses you. We've all had that experience of writing a paper or doing something right before the deadline. We procrastinated until it was time to get going. To get into a focused "zone".

Not that I'm advocating procrastination, however, the deadline is what pushes and drives the action.

I actually had a situation one time where I wanted to register for an extremely expensive seminar, and I didn't know where the money could come from.

Finally, I just let go of the "how" and got really clear on all the details -- which event I wanted to go to, when I needed the money by, how much, and so on.

Much to my shock, someone actually gifted the money to me for my birthday, one week before the event started. Perfect timing!
So what I gave in return for that money was gratitude for my birthday gift, as that person would have given me something else instead. It was still an exchange.

Step 4: Create a well-defined plan to carry out your desire. More importantly, it's that you *begin* once your plan is set -- whether you're ready or not. That's crucial -- you must get started in carrying out the plan. It's about taking that first step, that first action and being willing to adjust the plan.

The first set of actions you take and what you learn might change the plan upside down. It might take you in a whole another direction, and that's okay. But starting is the key and then you continue to make sure that you focus on what you want throughout the process.

Step 5: Write out a clear and concise statement of everything. This is critical. You write "I want," "I have," "I will," "I will have," "I have now this amount of money for [whatever you want] by this date" or better.

By the way, I always add the phrase -- "or better" -- at the end of anything that I put into writing.

So when I wrote out what I wanted in a relationship, I wrote down things I wanted in that relationship and things I wanted in that man, and then I wrote at the very end "or better." For me, it gives life an opportunity to give me something better than I can possibly imagine.

Step 6: Re-read your statement. This is critical. Read your statement. Create a vision board with magazines and pictures of what you want and look at it every day. Read it in the morning, and read it at night before you go to bed.

It doesn't have to be a physical vision board, it can be a simple PowerPoint presentation or an online collage. This is so easy and fun to create.

You could make it your desktop background so you see it every time you sit down at your computer.

There are also many great programs and apps for this, just don't get hung up too much on the technology and make sure you actually do something.

It's really important to continually remind yourself of why you're doing what you're doing. Because as we said, the excitement may come and go, however connecting to your purpose for doing things will keep your enthusiasm spirit alive.

Bonus Step -- Let It All Go

Earlier, we said there were six steps to turning desires into reality. But I want to add what I call the bonus step, number seven. And that step for me is letting it go.

This is a subtle step, but I find it to be very profound. Because anytime you hold onto something so tightly, it feels suffocated.

In a sense, your goal is like raising a child. And when you're raising a child, you teach, you put love and attention into that child. Yet eventually you have to let that child go out in the world and come back to you.

Sometimes they'd come back to you all scraped up, and sometimes they come back to you all excited. And sometimes they come back to you emotionally hurt from whatever happened at school. It's really hard as a parent. I don't even have children myself, but I've been a child and also talked to enough parents to know how challenging it can be.

But you still have to let them go in order to grow. If you just kept them in a small little closet the rest of their lives, they would never grow mentally or physically, emotionally, or spiritually. They would never grow as a human being.

And that's the same thing for you - turning your dreams in realities. It's focusing on what you want, following the process and then letting go and trusting that you have done and are doing all the actions that you can.

Final Thoughts From a Sexy Boss

It's crucial that you find your fire, the place of burning hot desire that resides within. This is not about what excites you, but rather, what you feel most passionate and enthusiastic about.

Once you have that clearly in mind, use the seven-step process to turn that burning desire into a reality.

Lastly, be sure you practice this! Because the process will be used later on as we move to higher, more ambitious goals for you as a Sexy Boss.

Be You. Be Real. Be Sexy Boss!

Chapter 6

Who Cares If They Think You're a Bitch?

"I'm tough, ambitious, and I know exactly what I want. If that makes me a bitch, okay." - Madonna

I'm strong and I don't care if that makes me a bitch.

And you should feel the same way.

Unfortunately, many women are caught in a catch-22 double standard. To be really strong in business, you have to be tough. And being a strong, tough woman sometimes makes you a bitch in other people's eyes.

Well, to that I have just two words: *Who cares?*

Are you going to live life on your heels, catering to the opinions and judgments of others, no matter how wrong? HELL NO! You better not.

Because they ARE wrong. Very wrong. Anyone who automatically says you're a bitch because you're a strong, powerful, sexy woman is an idiot. And not worth listening to.

So again, who cares what they think?

The Real Source of Your Strength As A Woman

There are two things that make you a strong woman in the highest sense of the word. I call them burning desire plus persistence. Another name for that is what I call attitude and effort.

Now, I want to make sure when I talk about persistence and effort, I don't just mean work. It's normal to associate or equate the two, thinking that persistence and effort is a lot of work.

But that's not necessarily the case. Persistence is what keeps you going through everything. And it's *always* necessary. No matter your age, your income, your background, your education level, success has two elements: 1) you must have a burning desire and... 2) the persistence needed to take continuous action.

Without persistence, burning desire looks like a wishy washy desire -- it won't last through all that must be overcome in order to achieve something big.

On the other hand, if there's no desire behind it and just persistence, you'll lack the energy and enthusiasm to really give yourself all to that goal or venture. Without either one, you'll just stay in the same place and never make real progress or forward movement.

So, I want to make sure that you understand these two elements as being part of being a Sexy Boss: It's this burning desire plus persistence action.

Breaking Free of Poverty Consciousness

Imagine you are driving down the road and you pull into a large parking lot to a Wal-Mart. We're here in America and there's pretty much a Wal-Mart in every town. So you walk into that Wal-Mart and you see people that work there. They're getting paid per hour and they're working hard.

And many of them, no disrespect to anyone who works at Wal-Mart, but many of them are working hard, taking action, and even persisting through their day. But there isn't a higher intention or ambition, there is not a burning desire to move beyond where they're at – and that is what I call a poverty consciousness.

Poverty consciousness is more of the average here in the United States than it is not the average. There's only a small portion of the population that is considered wealthy. They have developed what I call "money consciousness".

And the reason why I call it consciousness is because it's not something we actually know is there until we start bumping up against it or wanting to change it. And as Sexy Bosses, it is our responsibilityto choose money consciousness in every moment.

And that takes effort, it takes a burning desire, and it takes persistence because so much of society pushes us in the direction of poverty consciousness.

Even from the time we enter college, we are too often pushed into a category of work that is "safe" and "secure" rather than doing something big or great. It's all around us -- from college professors to TV to magazines and beyond.

Yes, even our magazines from *Smart Money* magazine to *Forbes* or others don't actually teach money consciousness. And part of being the Sexy Boss is choosing to wake up and choosing to know that what you were taught from the beginning - from school, parents, elders – most likely is not money consciousness. Just because you've saved money does not necessarily mean you have a money consciousness. I'm going to give you an example from my own life.

The Ghosts of Financial Past

I was on my own by the time I was 17. I had my first 401K by that age. In fact, I remember when I walked into the American Express Financial Advisers office and they said "Wow, you're quite young to have a financial adviser." And I said, "Well, I'm interested."

My desire at that point in my life was to learn at an early age how to create wealth. I had come from a family that had had wealth and had lost it all. I have lived in both wealth and in poverty. And I was making a decision. I was not going to live in poverty anymore. That was the burning desire.

So at age of 20 years old, I become a client. I wrote a personal check to this financial planner and I began to plan and I begin to save. No matter what job I had, I saved 10% of my income even if I was waiting tables, working as a hostess, or then getting a corporate job at the age of 21. I saved. And I was a great client.

At one point, I actually started working at American Express Financial Advisers as you learned last chapter. And at that point I started to learn what financial advising was all about. And what I learned was that their job as financial advisers was to sell people on certain products and services.

Basically they were just services or investment tools -- such as mutual funds, annuities, insurances and so on – that they got a commission on.

Now, nothing is wrong with that. All those things are valuable. However, what I learned was their clients not necessarily were getting wealthier. They weren't teaching money consciousness.

They were actually teaching them poverty consciousness because they weren't fully helping them leverage their wealth. They might be getting their 10% at the end of the year. Heck, they might even get a 20% return at the end of the year if it was a good year.

But that doesn't mean that they were creating and helping people have actual money consciousness. Investment tools are great, but they are NOT money consciousness success tools. Sometimes these financial instruments actually kept clients in poverty consciousness! Because the advisers would sell them a product or a service for their own benefit, and not that of the client.

As a Woman, Breaking Free From Poverty Consciousness May Be Even More Challenging

You may be wondering why I'm talking about money consciousness in a chapter that is titled, "Who Cares If They Think You're a Bitch?"

However, I'm doing this as a warning to you. Because once you become very powerful with money as a woman -- there's an even greater chance you'll be perceived as a bitch. It's almost inevitable. Almost every powerful, wealthy woman has been called a bitch at one time or another, simply by virtue of the power that she wields.

However, once you understand this, you can be prepared.

Remember that having the money consciousness is a personal responsibility, no one is going to teach you unless you go out and actively seek the right Big Boy in Business advice.

You pay for that information. No one's going to knock on your door and tell you about it, not a magazine, nothing. You've got to go out and find the right kind of information that's going to teach you how to have a money consciousness, just like you've done with this book.

And it's up to you to make the right choices in everyday situations. If not, our society will automatically pull you in the direction of poverty consciousness.

As you get stronger as a Sexy Boss and more clear, you'll gain momentum and the whole thing becomes easier and more lucrative.

Labels Don't Mean Anything, You Create Your Own Meaning

One thing you'll notice is that those who are quickest to label or judge you in a certain way are often the most envious. This is true whether they criticize you or anyone else.

They might see Madonna doing her thing, get jealous, and pick at her in some way. But it's really their issue, Madonna is actually living fully as a Sexy Boss -- the person sitting back and criticizing is not.

This is the same type of person that's often not willing to take that first step to start that new business, to start that new franchise, to step out and start that college career they always wanted, whatever it is. They are scared and it's easy to sit back and just criticize and label others.

Again, just ignore them. There are endless challenges in this path, and the naysayers are just one of many.

This is why, in a world of Sexy Boss, salesmanship is critical. Salesmanship not only of yourself but also of the situation and where you're going. And what I mean by selling is that you've got to sell yourself personally and internally.

I honestly have to sell myself every day and reassess my life... always making sure I'm on the right track every moment by moment.

Sometimes when I am writing I have to resell myself on why I'm doing it. I check in with myself and connect to that burning desire. If I let the naysayers and critics get in my head, I'll never have that persistence. So I sell myself on why it's important for me to be doing what I'm doing.

"Holding Back" Only Hurts You and Others Around You

Where women fall in the world of sales is that they are good at selling the company's product or service, but not at selling themselves. I see this even with the top saleswomen at the biggest corporations.

They may be able to sell more than any man in the company when it comes to the products or services offered. However, when it comes to presenting and selling themselves -- this is where their self-confidence as a women becomes completely faulty and they don't do well. It's generally not their strength.

It's weird because women are taught not to talk about themselves, not to focus on themselves, but to help other people. And of course, focusing on other people helps women do well in a sales environment.

But again, let's say the woman quits her sales job and wants to start a new company. Now, when she's in front of a group of investors and selling this group of investors on why they should put money into her company, that is a completely different story. She loses part of her excellent sales ability.

Part of the challenge is that as a woman, when you promote or sell yourself (including your own personal company or project), you risk coming across as a bitch. But for a man, it's a big weakness if you can't sell yourself.

So men learn this more easily and at a younger age, but as women we often have externally imposed limitations that become ingrained within, if we're not careful.

That's why, as a Sexy Boss woman going after extraordinary success, you'll often need to have extra persistence within yourself.

Once your persistence is truly boundless, you can more easily go out and be a salesperson and promote yourself -- including who you are, and everything you're doing.

Sure people may say, "What a bitch!" But again, that's their problem, not yours.

You see this a lot even in today's world in politics. Women who are extremely strong in politics no matter what side they're on, Democrat or Republican, are perceived as "bitches" more than men are labeled as "jerks" or "assholes".

If you've ever experienced that, don't feel bad. Actually, it's a great thing, because it's your opportunity to say...

"To Hell With The Status Quo!"

Now you have the opportunity to look at everything with fresh eyes, even if it absolutely flies in the face of the status quo.

Even in our "modern world" as we call it where women go to school, go to college, thrive in companies, pretty much do anything, we are still taught at a very young age to "be strong but don't be a bitch". Or "be a good little girl" or "be sweet or be loving".

But when you're six-years old and you're a little girl, they'll teach you to be passive, to be extra sweet, to cater to others, be a good little girl, and in school and society you are rewarded for that behavior.

What do they say to little boys? "Be strong," "Don't cry," "You can do it" – completely different kinds of messages. To the boy, they'll say "Go, be strong," "Go fight for what you want," "Go after what you want."

The little girl was told "Now, now. Don't go after the toy that you want. Be nice," "Share," "Don't do that," "Let's share what you have" – it's deeply ingrained in society.

So of course females will grow up into that society that tells them "Be strong. Be strong, little girl, but don't be a bitch." But then men who are strong and maybe territorial and maybe kind of a jerk but they're successful, we give them glamour and recognition.

They are men that women want to be with. They're someone that attracts women, that lands the high paying jobs, that gets success because they're strong and independent and everything men are "supposed" to be. But a woman does all the same things – independent, strong, powerful, focused, self-reliant, makes her own money – and she's a bitch.

Now, this is not happening everywhere across the board -- it's actually slowly changing.

But I want to make sure the distinction here is about being strong on who you are, being confident in who you are, and what you're going after. And there's a different energy about it to be able to be focused, to be confident, to be centered, connected, and be the boss of your own life. Also to be 100% responsible for having the money consciousness.

Make This Fundamental Shift In Your Being, The Rest Of Your Life Will Flow

You're naturally born persistent. I think we are naturally born to survive. It's an innate part of a human being in the planet. I don't think that we are trained to be persistent because I actually think laziness is a learned or trained behavior.

Someone who is lazy was not born that way. That's trained behavior. So I want to make sure you know that training yourself to be persistent is a muscle, just like you train yourself in the gym.

There are actually five key steps to help build your persistence as a business woman and as a Sexy Boss.

1) State of mind. Persistence is something you choose to do at the moment by moment basis. Being persistent in going after what you want in life. It could be just being persistent in going after you want a particular hotel versus another hotel. Someone tells you "No," and you don't take that "No."

You go after what you want. It can be something as simple as that. It really is a state of mind.

> *"Your goal should be out of reach but not out of sight." - Anita DeFrantz, Olympic Rower*

2) Having a definite purpose. When you're going after something extremely large -- something that pushes and stretches who you are, then it requires a purpose.
You've got to have that burning desire coupled with a strong reason why (purpose) that drives you in doing that. You may want that new job not just for the money but also for the feeling it's going to bring you. The challenge or the deeper sense of satisfaction you'll feel from it.

3) Burning desire. By desire, I mean literally like a fire burning inside of us. There's something inside of us that says "Where you're at now is not where you need to be." You have a desire, a burning in your heart or in your gut, to go somewhere, to move, and that desire is something that you can choose to have or you can snuff it out. A lot of people snuff it out. They ignore it. But not you. You are a Sexy Boss.

4) Self-reliance. Now self-reliance is critical. It's different than confidence. Self-reliance is that knowing that you are reliant on who you are and you're reliant on one's self. Now, you might be in the real world "dependent" financially or dependent on a job or a situation or a person.

But that doesn't mean you're not self-reliant. Self-reliance really is the knowing who you are, who you want to be, and where you're headed. It's that calmness in the storm.

5) Definite plan. Wishing that you want to start a new business, wishing that you want to go after your Olympic dreams, without a definite plan is like a broken car. It says "How are you going to get from A to B when you don't have a map, you don't have a road, and your car is broken down?" You have to have the definite plan.

Sexy Boss Always Has a Clear, Definite Plan

A definite plan is definitely something I have failed with in the past. I just went with the flow. I went where people wanted me to go or I followed the plan of others. I do a very good job of following the plans of other people.

I've been in situations at events and seminars, workshops, organizations, college where people give me a plan of how this semester or how the six-week workshop is going to go and I followed that thing to a "T".

But when I think of my own dreams and where I want to go and someone goes "Great! What are your plans?" I just go "Oops! I don't know." And then I wake up four years later and I don't have the dreams I want.

Why is that? I did not have a definite plan and that is a critical piece. If you look at our society, this is really critical, we are taught from the age of six years old to wake up at a certain time, get ready for school, mom took you, and then you had a teacher and the teacher told you what to do.

Everything was planned for you. And it's the same thing in virtually every job.

However, the moment that we actually create something totally new and outside of that box -- which you'll be doing as a Sexy Boss -- that's where everything changes and you need to be able to create your own plan.

As soon as you set out to start your own business or company, and you need to learn how to bring in money on your own -- you must be able to create a plan, follow it, and then always be adjusting it on the fly. We are not taught that, ever, and it's something that's extra important for you to learn.

Especially as a woman. Because nobody is going to make it easy for you, I promise. It's up to you to plan for what you want, and then take it, even if that makes you the biggest bitch in the world.

Just like the Madonna quote we began with, you say: *"If that makes me a bitch, okay."*

Final Thoughts from a Sexy Boss

When you're a strong, powerful, sexy woman—some people may call you a bitch. Who cares! You can't live your life according to what other people think. And the sooner you realize that, the better.

Once you fully reclaim your power, and approach your life with both burning desire and persistence, you can have anything you want. And most importantly, whatever you do get will have deep meaning for you.

Chapter 7

Making the No BS Decision To Turn Pro

"TURNING PRO IS FREE, BUT IT'S NOT EASY. When we turn pro, we give up a life that we may have become extremely comfortable with. We give up a self that we have come to identify with and to call our own." -- Steven Pressfield

When you're ready to take money-making seriously, it's time "turn pro".

Of course, I'm not just talking about money here… but actually cashing in on something you're truly passionate about.

I'm guessing that you have something you love, but at the same time, you're an amateur at doing what you love. Or perhaps you've created a business and "gone pro" – just not all the way.

Well, let's clarify… going pro means playing at 100%, going all the way.

Let's say you're very good at writing lyrics, just as a hypothetical.

There is a moment when you have to ask yourself, is this something you want to do with their life? Can you spend years or even decades writing lyrics?

It might not be what you went to school for. You don't have a class called "How to write songs for record label companies" in college or even high school.

So the first thing to talk about in a discussion about turning pro is that pivotal moment when you decide to pursue something. Ideally, it's something you can be "great" at -- it's a place where you have natural skill and burning desire.

Amateur Versus Pro, Which Are You?

Yes, there should always be a moment when you actually know there's both skill and burning desire to pursue something.

Now, you can't be a pro at everything. Maybe a couple things, maximum. The rest you'll be an amateur and that's okay. The problem is when you act like an amateur in an area where you should really be a pro.

Let me explain. In the amateur life, a person is easily distracted. They still follow what I call the moralistic model, which is very conventional thinking. They feel that their skill or desire doesn't have much value in the business world.

And they don't pursue it seriously.

If you've ever heard, "Oh, I do this thing on the side," or "Yeah, I write a few songs when I can on the side". They play with the thing on the side, like a little kitten playing with a ball of string. When they have time, when they feel like it, they play.

And they usually don't ask for money for it. Some people I know who are really good at massage, they just give massages. They don't even think to consider to actually go get paid for what they love. They just enjoy giving it, and that's being an amateur.

Which can be fine, even beautiful that someone just does something just for love or enjoyment. But in most cases, the person would actually love to be a professional at song writing or massage -- but they don't take the risk or put all their chips "in" and pursue that 100% as a pro.

The person could say, "Well, I'm really good at sketching things. I'm going to put myself in a local competition," of the county, local city, or state. Maybe they even won and yet, still, they don't position themselves as pro. They have an amateur mindset.

It's also being in the mindset that something is usually wrong with their skill set.

There Is NOTHING Wrong With You – Stop Whining

During our time as amateurs, it's easy to feel or think that something is wrong with us or the world or our parents. Some might go to therapy for years to figure out what's wrong or they might pursue a particular religion or a particular self-improvement seminar. And they'll do this to see if they can fix themselves or figure out where they should go in life.

However, when one turns pro, he or she finds power inside and becomes a true Sexy Boss. And this person just moves forward, not waiting until everything is perfect or "fixed".

The problem is that being stuck in the "process of transformation" can sometimes be addictive, like a drug. There's a high that comes from the feeling that you've figured out what's wrong with you and can now move forward. For many, this repeats itself over and over again.

Personally, I've done it all. I'm happy to say that I've done all the above to the extreme. I went to therapy two days a week for almost four years. I was involved in a church. I attended about four to five days a week for a few years. I was involved in a personal development seminar company. I did that about three or four days a week for five years.

So I'm not pointing the finger at anyone. I've looked for a really long time, trying to figure out what was "wrong with me".

As I finally got to the end of that road, I began to uncover my real passion -- which is teaching marketing and lifestyle to woman internationally about how to be their best, by awakening the Sexy Boss within. This is what I can be great at.

This is my calling. Then one day I drew a line in the sand and turned pro.

I didn't leave all my experiences behind. I don't think anything is wrong with me going through all those experiences. However, I'll say that finding my calling and turning pro have made that search less relevant -- I don't need it anymore.

I know who I am, what I was put here to do, and why it means so much to me.

Remember also, that everyone has their own journey. I feel some people go to India or they live in India and they do meditation. Everyone has their own journey in terms of how they're going to figure out what their calling is.

Sometimes they find that when they're 20, 30, 40 or 50 years old. Just know that you turning pro could be a small step today.

Why Being a Sexy Boss Is Not For Everyone

So first I must say that turning pro and being 100% Sexy Boss is not for everyone. Everyone can do it; however, I will say again that it's not for everyone.

Now, what I mean by that is as Stephen Pressfield says in his book *Turning Pro*:

"What we get when we turn pro is we find our power. We find our will and our voice and we find our self-respect. We become who we always were but had, until then, been afraid to embrace and live out."

So let me repeat what I was trying to say is that turning pro happens in a moment, but it's not for everybody. Everyone can do it, but it's not for everyone. It is when our higher spirit emerges with our mind and they connect. That's when we draw a line in the sand of our lives and we take forward action that causes us to remember that moment forever.

Now, what I mean by that is that we always remember the first dollar you made once you've decided to turn pro. It's THE big day when, after hours of practice and learning, that someone actually pays you for your work.

Turning pro is something that you choose to do in that moment and once that line is drawn, you can never go back.

Many times if you fly into L.A. or even New York and you see people go, *"Oh, I'm an actor,"* *"Oh, I'm an actress,"* and then you go, *"What do you do every day?"*

"Well, I wait tables" or *"I bartend."* *"Well, how many auditions have you gone to this week?"* *"None."* *"How many auditions have you gone to this month?"* *"Oh, I just haven't had the time."*

Not to be harsh, but those in this position are not who they say they are.

Everybody Great Makes the Decision to Go Pro At Some Point

Turning pro is not always easy, it takes sacrifice.

In the case of the waitress, she knows she'd be good at it, yet she often keeps using the distraction of other things, people, social life, just getting by financially as reasons she hasn't turned pro yet.

But unfortunately, until she draws the line in the sand, that day will never come. Because I promise you the day that George Clooney, Catherine Zeta-Jones, Julia Roberts made the decision to go pro, they might have been broke in that moment, but that was the moment things started to turn around for them.

It's when they started to think of themselves as a pro actress or a pro actor in the world. Whenever you do that, things change and move forward. It's inevitable.

Trust me, before Michael Phelps ever even got to his fourth Olympics, he already made the decision that he was a pro. He already made that decision before he got his first Olympic medal. Swimming was the most serious thing on the planet for him.

One of the things that turning pro does is it actually causes you to turn yourself into a real professional. My life changed when I allowed myself to turn pro as a speaker, author and writer.

I allowed myself to stop chasing after every job that I was supposed to be doing or supposed to be good at. I stopped listening to what others had to say on what my life should look life. I also stopped what I call 'trying to be saved.'

Turning Pro Does Not Mean Being Fixed, Saved Or Transformed

Let me say that again. Being saved or being fixed or being transformed does not mean you're happy, does not mean that you're making money, and does not mean that you're a pro. It just means you're saved. It just means you're fixed to another person's standards.

It has nothing to do with you fully choosing to be a pro in terms of what you do every day with your life. It actually has nothing to do with you making money either. It has nothing to do with you being a Sexy Boss and being the owner of how your life goes.

So going back, turning pro and choosing being a professional in an area where you have both talent and a burning desire -- is up to you to figure out.

It could be being a professional writer, a professional basketball player, anything...

There's actually a guy named Adam Richman and he has a TV show called, *Man Versus Food*. And that's what he does for a living -- he goes to restaurants known for amazingly rich/heavy food with huge portion sizes, and he often pushes himself to see if he can eat the whole thing. It could be a four pound hamburger, or a five pound plate of nachos, or huge sandwich. It changes every time.

But the point is, he's crystal clear that he's a professional at it. The show is entertaining and very successful -- it's been running for years. It sounds crazy but by our definition, he's a professional at it. He makes money by going around the world doing something he's incredibly passionate about.

As we learned eariler, being fixed or being saved according to another person's standards has nothing to do with you making money. It has nothing to do with you being a Sexy Boss and being the owner of your life.

Turning pro has everything to do with you choosing that your vocation is something of value and professional -- and treating that with the utmost seriousness.

Example, writing this book is an action of my turning pro. This is not my hobby. This is not something I do on weekends and Friday nights. This is my life. This is my turning pro. The line has been crossed for me, and I'm writing, creating and developing the Sexy Boss process because it is the way I choose to live my life.

Starting Your Own Business Around What You Love

First of all, if you want to build a great business, don't do it as a hobby.

Let me give an example. A friend of mine loves and is very good at creating pickles. She puts them in jars, and she labels them, and she gives them away to friends in their special hot sauce. She calls them all different fun names.

There's all these different ways to create really good pickles versus the ones you get at the store. She's seriously good at this.

Now, what's interesting about it is she finally got the mindset of, "I can create pickles and create a pickle company." Now, not like a local pickle company just like locally in Texas but really she could actually sell her recipe to pickle companies and have them manufacture different kinds of pickles under her brand. So she's doing that.

She's getting a graphics guy to create a whole new look and feel and brand. She's working with a local manufacturing company to be able to develop the recipe. And then she's contacting large chain grocery stores as well as food brokers to see how she can actually create a pickle company.

This is truly a business, not a hobby. If she wants to create a hobby, she throws some pickles in a jar, she sets her little booth up at the local Farmer's Market and there she is; she has this little hobby on the side.

That's not what she wanted to do. If she's going to make this a business and it's something she's very good at. This can be a multi-million dollar business and she knows it.

There was a clear moment when she turned pro and began to think of herself as a professional businesswoman. A creator of a professional pickle company.

Two Specific Actions That Help You Turn Pro

Turning pro is a decision point; yet it's also a process. Here's how it works:

Step 1: Recognition. By this I mean recognizing that you have value in an area where you can fully dedicate yourself, and earn money from it. Everything we've discussed still applies -- you must also have skill or talent, burning desire and persistence.

Step 2: Make the decision to take that pursuit on full-time. Or as much as humanly possible. Of course, I realize that if you've got bills, you may need to work two jobs until your new business or new career is evolved enough to stand on its own and let you do it full time. That's okay, you can still be a pro without working 40+ hours.

The key is your level of dedication.

When you're totally honest with yourself, you instantly know if you're 100% dedicated to something or not. It's something you just feel.

So it might be that waitress who says, "I really want to become an actress. I want to turn pro. I promise that every week I'm going to go to one or two at least auditions." That is an action which shows they are serious about turning pro. If they are a writer of songs, as we discussed, they actually are picking up the phone and sending their songs to a record company every week, or producing a certain number of songs each month and developing a plan to market or sell them.

I want to give you another quote from Stephen Pressfield, and here is the quote:

"The difference between amateur and a professional is in their habits. An amateur has amateur habits; a professional has professional habits. We can never free ourselves from habits. The human being is a creature of habit. But we can replace bad habits with good ones. We can train in the habits of the amateur and the addict for the practice of the professional and the committed artist or entrepreneur."

The Unparalleled Power Of Simplicity

On top of added income and wealth, there's another big benefit to turning pro -- simplicity. Because life gets really simple when you turn pro.

It's when you're an amateur and addicted to a bunch of different things that your life gets more complicated and more dramatic. If you look at people that are professional at something, anything -- actress, attorney, writer, nutritionist, personal trainer -- it doesn't matter what it is. When they are a professional, their life is extremely simple and so much more in control and stable.
When someone is in chaos personally, their life is chaos. There's a lot of drama and personal pain that comes along. There's a lot of ego in their life. I know that for a fact. I've been there.

The moment I turned pro my life got really clear. Now, it doesn't get easy; it just got clear. It's not all of a sudden everything came to me 100% like I just got clear on what I'm here to do.

Thus, your job as a person and as a Sexy Boss is to figure out what you're here to do because once you get that, everything else will fall into place over time. The universe will test you to make sure that your commitment is real and 100%.

That's when the flow will actually happen. Even as an entrepreneur, even as an actress, there will be challenges. But no matter what the challenges are, that actress knows she's an actress, that entrepreneur knows she's an entrepreneur.

This is just part of the road. That lawyer knows she might have lost that case, but she is still a lawyer the next day.

And remember, failures are just a test. The surgeon might have lost somebody on the surgeon table. They might have lost somebody and that's painful, but he or she doesn't stop being a surgeon the next day. It's part of the profession.

Like an NFL player, they may lose the big game. They may even lose the Super Bowl. Yet they're still an NFL player the next year, and they deal with that loss like a professional.

An amateur will experience drama around it. But as a pro, as much as it may hurt, you get on with it and resolve to be better next time. That's all you can do.

In this sense, life becomes extremely simple and you gain more momentum and power as a Sexy Boss when you have that level of simplicity and clarity underlying your overall mission.

So Much More To Come!

When it comes to being a Sexy Boss and making money doing something you love, this is only the beginning.

There's a lot more that I'm going to be sharing with you – especially regarding finding your strengths, choosing a business model, the nitty gritty of building your business and more.

It's not easy, of course. Things are only "easy" in infomercials and Disney movies. You will have to work at it, and be focused about it. That's why I've placed such an emphasis here on going pro.

The good news is that you're already farther than most women ever get, and with the tools you're about to discover, you can experience success most others can't even dream about.

Final Thoughts From a Sexy Boss

Anyone who ever did something great has made the clear decision to "turn pro" at one point in their life. You are no different.

To have the life you want, it's imperative you find out what you love, learn how to make money with it, and then dedicate yourself with effort and smart strategies.

Turning Pro in business is turning pro in your life. Life becomes clear and things begin to fall into place.

Your life will change forever the day you choose to turn Pro.

Chapter 8

Step Into the Spotlight And Change Your Life

"You may have a fresh start any moment you choose, for this thing that we call 'failure' is not the falling down, but the staying down." - Mary Pickford 1893-1979, Actress and Producer

Being a Sexy Boss means being willing to be seen.

It means not shying away from attention – and stepping out into the spotlight.

No more hesitating, no hiding in the back of the room. If you want to be everything you can be as a Sexy Boss, you must be willing to seize the opportunity to actively step into the spotlight.

Are you afraid of what people think about you? Do you dread the thought of having other people focusing on you? If so, what you're about to learn will be life-changing.

Because too many people say, "I don't want others to focus on me. I'm not that selfish."

Or they say words like "I don't want the focus to be on me. I don't want to be in the spotlight. I just want to help people."

But those are just fears masquerading as altruism. Which is BS as you might guess. You are not helping anybody by sitting quietly in the back of the room.

Being the "Center of Attention" Is NOT Stepping Into the Spotlight

It's easy to think that stepping into the spotlight makes you some sort of attention whore, but that's not what I'm saying here.

Stepping into the spotlight is getting over your fears and finding the courage to be the one who people look to, trust and rely on. It's being the face and the leader people learn from.

It doesn't mean you have to be egotistical and be the center of attention. That is not the real meaning of "the spotlight".

It's often about not being submissive and not afraid. Because being a leader and director means being willing to be seen, inspiring trust and confidence in others.

And you can't do that if you're hiding.

I have seen situations where you have a predominant lawyer or doctor and they have an assistant – a nurse or a paralegal – that they lean on for many, many things. But you'll rarely if ever see that paralegal in the courtroom. Or that nurse in the surgery room.

Does that nurse or paralegal have what it takes to be in the spotlight -- to be the surgeon or lawyer? Often times, yes. However, early on they made a conscious decision to not step up and be into the spotlight.

If that person is okay with being the nurse or paralegal, that's okay. However, if they want more -- there is conflict and they will push up against their personal resistance to step into the spotlight.

Of course, being in the spotlight is not about being domineering or controlling others. It's about putting yourself on the line, letting others see you and be guided by your strength.

When you step into the spotlight in an authentic way, the whole process feels natural and not like excessive control or domination.

The Secret to Performing Under Pressure

Have you ever seen the movie *Tin Cup* with Kevin Costner?

He is an amazing golfer in the film. However, he's never played in the big leagues. He's never been on the pro golf tour. So he's this phenomenal golfer who just hangs out and doesn't live up to his potential.

He's not being the amazing golfer that he could be. So he hires a psychologist to talk about his mind and how he can start realizing his full greatness on the golf course.

The problem is, whenever he's under pressure or "in the spotlight" -- he chokes. He is still the same amazing golfer but he just can't perform under pressure.

Yet, by working through all this with his therapist -- he learns to break through and perform under pressure. He figures it out. He realizes how and why he's afraid to really step into the spotlight and be great. And everything changes.

If you currently have any fears that cause you to (metaphorically) sit hidden in the back of the class, it's up to you to figure out why those fears are there -- and move beyond them. I'm going to give you some insights and tools in this chapter to make that process easier, but ultimately it will be up to you to do the work.

Get Out of Your Head!

A big part of the problem is over-thinking or something I call "being stuck in your head". Because more often than not, thinking breeds worry and causes you to choke or fail in moments that require decisive action.

The clearest, most decisive actions occur when your mind is clear and quiet -- not cluttered with a bunch of thoughts. Because thoughts are often by nature contradictory. They move in different directions, mean different things, distracting you from what needs to be done.

Just think of a tightrope walker in the circus. This person is walking hundreds, sometimes thousands of feet above the ground. There is a net, but the height is still very scary. And they have 200,000 people staring at them at the same time.

That is intense pressure. And thinking about the people, or what they think, or the risk, the height, the fall or anything else is NOT helpful to the situation.

The only thing that truly serves them in that moment is focusing on the rope, their balance and each step. The actual actions required to get across.

So many key moments in life are like that -- we know what to do, but we get into our heads, over-analyze and think excessively about irrelevant details that simply don't allow us to act with strength.

This is the key to performing under pressure.

My Story – Learning from A Young Age

Let me give you an example of my life. I was brought up in a home always in crisis, so I learned how to deal with crises situations at a very young age.

In fact, it became so commonplace that when things were calm and peaceful it just felt weird to me.

So because of this, high pressure situations have always been easy.

Of course, there were times -- as we've covered -- when I

had such an intense crisis that it took me a long time to recover. As in the case where my business and money was taken away from me.

Still, even then, I was able to regroup and rebuild my life without spending huge amounts of time or energy trying to get revenge -- or wallow in pity.

I began to realize that all the thoughts and mental clutter can make or break you in these moments. The sooner I just ignored the mental "chatter" in my head and took decisive action in the direction of rebuilding my life how I wanted it, I began to be supported in many amazing ways.

So if you react properly at crisis, it can give you strength and power and wisdom you do not ordinarily possess.

If you react improperly, a crisis can rob you of skills, control, and your ability to take action in a forward direction. So here are some steps you can take to better perform under pressure...

3 Ways To Turn Crisis Into Power

Use this process to accelerate your ability to step into the spotlight and perform under pressure:

Step #1: Learn crucial skills under conditions where there will be pressure -- but first *without* pressure. So in other words, you practice without pressure.

If you're a tightrope walker, this would mean practicing walking across the rope at a lower height so that you train your body and mind -- without the immense risk and pressure you'd normally face.

If you're going to be speaking in public, first practice your speech alone in the mirror, then in front of a small group of friends. Start in lower pressure situations, so that you can build your comfort and muscle-memory with less on the line.

This gives you something to actually rely on when the pressure is on in the big moment.

Step #2: Learn to react to crisis with an aggressive rather than a defensive attitude. This means responding to the challenge of the situation assertively, while keeping your positive goal in mind. Don't wait for a resolution, CREATE the resolution you want. Seize the moment. Don't sit back and hope things go your way. They usually won't.

Think of a firefighter. When there is an emergency, they must remain calm and poised, yet they have to be incredibly decisive and move fast. They have to be the aggressor... if they wait, if they're passive, people will die. It's really clear.

Many moments in your life are not life or death like this, but they are pivotal. They can either move you forward, or slowly kill your dreams and goals.

By acting assertively and decisively, you not only keep them alive and help turn them into reality.

Step #3: Learn to evaluate so-called crises situations in their truest perspective. This will help you avoid making a mountain out of a molehill, or reacting as if some small challenge were a matter of life or death.

Now, just because I said to be aggressive in a crisis situation doesn't always mean "attack." It could just mean having a strong, proactive mindset. Or being willing to instantly act at any moment.

This step is about being able to pause and say, *"What's really going on here? What is the REAL problem here?"*

And then looking at it with a strong, clear, unbiased perspective.

Sometimes the best action you can take is no action at all. Or a different action than the one everyone is telling you to take. Counter-intuitive.

Again, as in the case of my lost business -- a 'normal' and dramatic reaction would have been to spend years battling my partners in court. But then what? Maybe I would have won, but there's no amount of compensation I could have received that would have taken the place of the 1-3 years lost in that process.

So in that case, taking no action against my partners -- and NEW action in the direction of rebuilding my life, was the best choice. And where I am now as a Sexy Boss proves that I made the right decision.

How To Build Confidence In the Spotlight, Even With Everything On the Line

Again, I can't overstate the importance of practice without pressure.

There is so much value in putting yourself into a situation where you are practicing what you ultimately want to be able to do under pressure.

If you are a public speaker and then you stand in front of the mirror and deliver your speech. It's been said that Steve Jobs used to practice his new product presentations dozens of times before they happened.

He'd practice at work, at home, and then rehearse multiple times at the actual venue. And it showed.

People assumed he was just a naturally great presenter and

salesman, but the fact was that his biggest secret was preparation.

And it showed. While the Apple products were usually not available to purchase at the time of his presentations, what he did on stage was a key ingredient in all the buzz, excitement and sales that followed.

And it showed. Apple has become the most valuable company in the history of the world, sold hundreds of billions of dollars in products, and much of it can be traced back to Steve's amazing presentations.

Sure, he had natural talent and skill in this area -- but it was also his incredible preparation (first done without any pressure) that allowed him to perform so well in the spotlight.

And the same will be true for you.

Practicing Puts Confidence In To Your Muscle Memory

Muscle memory is important, but it takes self-confidence to execute on the practice you've put in. Let's go back to Tin Cup for a moment.

He had practiced his strokes over and over and over. It had nothing to do with his muscle memory. It was his mental response to the pressure of the people watching that made his muscle memory disappear.

He had played that same course a thousand times and done well, yet his muscle memory failed in the pressure of the situation.

When an Olympian swims a particular event, they've probably done that exact same stroke and distance thousands times. In some cases, tens of thousands of times. Performance is mental at that point, because the strokes are ingrained in their muscle memory.

So muscle memory is not enough. It also comes down to belief.

Peak performers always believe that they'll perform under pressure -- even right after they fail. The basketball player Kobe Bryant could miss 20 shots in a row and still 100% believe that he's going to make the last shot to win the game.

It was the same with Michael Jordan and any great performer.

But how do you develop belief in yourself? That's a big question -- for now, let's just cover a few actions you can take.

Sexy Boss Exercise

1) Affirmations. Write out what you want to believe about yourself. That is your affirmation. Best to start out with the words, "I AM..." and then whatever belief you want to have.

For example, you say: "I AM a confident, charismatic speaker."

That is your affirmation. Repeat that in your mind as much as possible, and even more powerfully, repeat it out loud in front of the mirror. Notice if you feel any discomfort or reluctance to accept that belief. Continue to say and repeat even after you feel 100% certain you ARE that.

2) Creative visualization. Another way to be more confident under pressure is to actually imagine yourself in pressure in intense detail -- performing the way you want to perform.

Make it real in your mind. See and feel yourself doing that *thing* with total confidence and *the* highest possible performance.

There's research that says your brain can't really distinguish between high-quality visualization and reality. For instance, one experiment with basketball players who visualized themselves making free throws (without actually practicing on the court) actually helped them outperform the guys who practiced only on the court!

Visualization is best done in a quiet place with no distractions.

Truth: Excitement is NOT Fear

It's normal to feel nervous or a little jittery right before a big moment. This isn't necessarily full blow fear. Don't interpret this feeling as a lack of confidence, because you're probably just excited.

Better yet, you can use it to propel yourself. So stop thinking in terms of fear and anxiety or nervousness. Think in terms of excitement. It's fine to be excited before you step into the spotlight in whatever you do. You can say, "Wow, I'm excited. Whoa, this is exciting!"

Another way to short-circuit any potential fear is to simply ask yourself: "Okay, what's the worst that possibly can happen?" Be rational about it.
Often fear is being in the unknown, but when you define the worst that can happen and you can mentally *accept* it, the fear loses its grip on you. And then if you still feel nervous or jittery, that's even more evidence that you're merely excited.

There is a LOT of energy in that nervous excitement. So use it. Let it direct your mind to a focused place, to a clear image of you winning or succeeding in the way that you've imagined.

I believe the very best performers all learned how to do this. Because everyone has that nervous energy and excitement during big moments.

But those who succeed most often are those who channel that energy into strong mental focus and determination to get the result they want.

As a Sexy Boss with big dreams, you'll find yourself in similar moments often.

Whether it's a crisis within your business, or a big moment presenting yourself and your business in front of others -- or maybe even appearing on TV -- you will need to handle pressure well.

And now you have more tools and strategies to do just that.

Thoughts from a Sexy Boss

It's okay to step into the spotlight. As a Sexy Boss, you will need to!

That doesn't mean you must be the center of attention all the time or a drama queen, but rather, a leader who others trust to make the right decisions at key moments.

Use the Sexy Boss exercise and tools to practice and grow your ability to perform under pressure. You'll notice a difference immediately. And you'll become a peak performer that others know will come through when it matters most.

Lastly, know that excitement is a way you can propel yourself. Be excited to step into the unknown!

Chapter 9

Girl Power and Being the Super Hero

Being a Sexy Boss is being a hero.

The hero's journey is the journey of every great superstar, every superman, superwoman. It is also the story of the courageous soldier, the dedicated mom who raised the kids, the successful entrepreneur, the list is endless.

The hero's story is really the backbone of every great movie we've ever seen from *Gone with the Wind* to *Slumdog Millionaire*.

As a Sexy Boss you can use the hero's journey to give greater meaning and understanding to your evolution. When you consciously develop yourself in this way, you avoid being swept into the negative stories and patterns pushed upon us by society.

This chapter will help you use the hero's journey to become even more powerful as a Sexy Boss and entrepreneur.

Be The Hero And Help Others Be The Sexy Boss

I feel that being the boss of our thoughts, our feelings, and our energy is being a hero for ourselves and everyone in our life.

Fundamentally, being the hero is being the leader.

Because only when we are hero for ourselves can we help other people.

When we embark on that heroic journey to go after our dream or our passion or what I call our art, we give other people the permission to do the same.

And it's crucial that you support and want the best for others, all the time. That is one of the first traits of the hero.

The question I sometimes I ask myself and pose to you now is: *"Are you thrilled about other people's abundance or are you jealous about other people's abundance?"*

Because when you're a Sexy Boss for yourself, you are your own hero and that in turn is helping other people realize who they are and go after their dreams.

You become a leader and a hero for people, old or young, no matter what.

Wishing Abundance for Others
Helps You Create It For Yourself

Again, the first inner step in being a hero is wanting the best for others, all the time. Are you thrilled about other people's success?

When you see someone driving around in a beautiful car that you might want, how do you feel? Or that house you want? Or maybe it's that beautiful horse that they have in their equestrian center... do you see it and feel jealous of them?

Are you envious of them? Or are you tapping into your Sexy Boss (your hero) inside, and actually thrilled that they have it?

Only villains are jealous.

The hero builds and creates moral support, whereas the opposite of hero, the villain, envies and creates destruction.

So you'll need to be honest with yourself. To observe how you really feel in the presence of success, and how you feel when others fail short. Be honest. Are you happy for people when you see what they have? Do you support people when they fall short?

Or are you secretly jealous of success -- and secretly happy when others fail?

As a Sexy Boss, I know you want the best for others. The fact that you've made it to this point in the book says you're a person of character.

Still, even the slightest bits of jealousy can poison us at times -- because the more clear we are in this area, the easier it is to be a great hero.

Telling The Naysayers To Shut Up

As we've learned, there will always be naysayers. The higher you go, the more people will attempt to invalidate or discredit you in some way.

This is especially true when it comes to money. Unfortunately, conventional wisdom often tells us that when one is wealthy, he or she is "taking" money out of the system. This is false. Money is energy, and as you and I grow and prosper, this gives access to others to prosper as well. There's no one taking money out of the system. Money is infinite.

When Bill Gates created Microsoft and became a billionaire, he didn't take the money out of the system. It was created exponentially for other people. Think of how massive the productivity and the wealth Microsoft created! And they did it by helping people use computers all over the world.

It's the same recently with Apple -- the wealth created by the explosion of the iPhone and iPad doesn't take money out of the system. Those products actually help people connect, grow and even excel in their lives and business. That value is wealth, and actually creates more wealth in the process.

So as you evolve in your journey of being Sexy Boss and, like the hero you go after what you want, you become more of everything. Nothing is taken from you or others.

You become more of the mother you want. You become the entrepreneur that you want. You become the online marketer that you want. You become more of everything you've ever wanted to be. You're adding value to everyone and the world at large, and therefore more value and wealth is coming back to you.

So when you see someone you know from a far distance or very close, send them joy and say to them, "I'm thrilled about your outrageous abundance." This gives them and you permission to accept your own abundance.

Beating the Villain Inside

It is not outside of us. Many people think that the villain is outside of us. There are so many things we can turn into a villain -- our spouse, possibly alcohol, drugs, sex addiction, drama. It might look like the villain is outside of us.

But the real hero's journey is overcoming the villain within.

The villain really is inside of ourselves. It's inside of our head. It's the self-sabotaging part of our minds that craves the excessive alcohol, or the drugs, or that tries to fill the void within us with sex or drama or causes fight with our spouses.

It's the villain inside of us that we need to understand that its job is to protect us from change and destroy good in us. The villain might look like something physical outside of us, but the job of the villain is to kill us, to kill our future, to kill our creativity, to kill love, to kill excitement, and to even kill our voice.

The hero's voice is different. It's consistent, it's quiet, and sometimes it's silent and you have to really listen to it. The villain's voice is a lot louder.

And as you grow through your hero's journey, as you become more of who you are and become a Sexy Boss, you'll begin to hear the difference between the villain and the hero.

Only a Quiet Mind Is Fully In Control

Building off what we covered last chapter, your ability to perform as a hero will depend on how well you're able to quiet your mind.

The quiet mind is the ability to put aside those random voices and that noise that swims around in our head. And it's like people saying, "Oh, I don't know where I got that thought."

But thoughts are a complex matter. One on hand, they're random and difficult to control. Hence how easy it is to over-think or be mentally clouded. On the other hand, thoughts are often a byproduct of your attention.

So if you put your attention on the wrong things -- like failure, what's wrong, what you don't want -- you'll have more of those thoughts. It's like the old Native American parable we uncovered about the wolves. The thoughts you have depend on which wolf you feed.

It takes a lot of mental noise and energy to keep us living small in this lifetime. It takes a lot of energy to keep that villain going. However, when your mind is quiet the villain is essentially dead -- he has no voice. Your hero is able to act freely because there is no noise interference.

Being a hero is often about listening to your higher self, even if you're not a religious or spiritual person. The term "higher self" just refers to that wiser, calmer more elevated part of you.

This is something that has taken me years and years to really understand, that the villain is not Heather.

The villain is something that wants to kill off the new Heather Ann, wants to kill off Sexy Boss. It doesn't want us to be our best and shine. Because being the hero, stepping out into the spotlight and shining is too risky to the ego.

Survival is everything to the ego, it wants safety first and above all else. However, when your mind is quiet and focused on moving forward, that villain has no power and in that moment your hero journey begins.

12 Stages In The Hero's Journey

When I was looking at doing research on this, I read a book called the *Hero's Journey*, by Joseph Campbell. He actually breaks down the hero's journey step by step. And what I find so fascinating about this is that we all go through it. We all have some kind of hero's journey within ourselves.

So here are the twelve stages of the Hero's Journey. Read closely you will find yourself somewhere in these stages, I guarantee you.

Stage 1: The Ordinary World

This is where you come from. Not necessarily your distant past, but your present. What your everyday ordinary world looks like.

This is important because every journey must have a beginning. Your present circumstances are part of what drive you to embark on the journey. So look closely at where you are in your life, not only where you live, but the state of various parts of your life.

Stage 2: The Call to Adventure

Next, you receive the call to adventure. You've probably already begun your journey someplace -- your journey to realize your greatness and design the life that you want. And that's fantastic.

However, you could argue that reading this book is your first step in the hero's journey of becoming a Sexy Boss. You've been called to adventure, to create something amazingly new and profound with your life.

Stage 3: Refusal of the Call

Next, the hero is reluctant. Maybe you heard the Sexy Boss message multiple times before you finally accepted the call and got started.

Or if your hero's journey is your business, I'm betting you had some initial moments where you ignored the call or doubted yourself. This is normal and happens almost anytime we aim for something that's much higher than what we might normally aspire to or out of our comfort zone.

Stage 4: Meeting With a Mentor

This is about encouragement. There should and will be someone in your life that directly or indirectly encourages you -- a mentor, a friend, a coach. It doesn't matter who it is, as long as you respect them and they can help you.

In this book, I'm the one helping you and encouraging you. When you launch your Sexy Boss business, it will be me and many others supporting and encouraging you.

Stage 5: Crossing the First Threshold

This is often right before the first test, a threshold you must cross to enter into a special world. Maybe it's one's first time as Olympian, first time public speaking or any other big moment in the journey.

This is crucial because it's what tests your resolve and perseverance and ability to move forward in the journey. In this stage, you strengthen your resolve.

In the Sexy Boss process, you might endure challenges in being the new you -- or launching your first business or something else that matters to you. And it's crucial that you cross this threshold and make it through to the other side.

Stage 6: Test, Allies, Enemies

This is when you and I encounter tests, allies, or enemies. It is the real ups and downs of the journey. As an entrepreneur, I remember when I first stepped into my threshold, in the thought leader world, the information marking world, I was so excited. I was also full of fear.

However, it's that moment that I began to be given tests, collect friends, discovered enemies, have businesses failed, create successes and much more. There were so many tests along the way.

You've already heard some of them, but just know and expect that you'll be tested in your journey. It will happen. Remember, you are a Sexy Boss and this all part of the journey toward greatness.

Stage 7: The Approach

This is where you approach the innermost cave crossing the second threshold. This is often when a person goes into a period of "incubation". In Jesus' journey, he went into the desert. In Oprah, she had a time in her life where nothing was really working.

It's a time when they go into a world where they endured an intense ordeal, meaning they endure the impossible. They begin a test that others simply don't think they can make it through.

It's about finding inner strength. Which brings us to...

Stage 8: The Ordeal

Now, they might have to go through suffering to get to there, but this stage is really about finding the inner strength to go beyond what people say is possible.

So for me I've had a few. One of them was after my personal business bankruptcy, after which I went into my cave. While in my cave I endured the whole process, including finding my own inner strength to move through it.

Ultimately, I went to the other side and to get to the other side I had to find the fire within me -- nobody could teach me that or give that to me. It was something I had to do.

Stage 9: The Reward

So the ordeal stage passed and now the hero experiences the rewards of surviving the stage. As the hero, when you've survived the 'death' stage, there's a whole another world that opens up.

Surviving that ordeal and death is really just the beginning. It is really the beginning of a whole new life. Remember, the big ordeal in your life could be anything -- it could be surviving cancer, it could be surviving a bankruptcy or surviving a divorce or moving through something you never thought you'd ever go through.

After that, on the other side of that process, is something new and rewarding. It could be a whole new career, an exploding business, a happy relationship, anything is open and possible at this stage.

Unfortunately, many people stop right before this happens. They just go through the pain. They go through the struggle. They never actually go through completely to the other side to reach the reward. The reward is the ability to go create what you want!

Sometimes The Lesson Is The Reward

I remember one day after my bankruptcy calling up a CEO of a major company that I used to work for, and setting up a meeting at Starbucks.

So we got there, and he was actually curious and surprised. "How can I help you?" he asked. So I point blank told him, "I actually created a business just like yours." And I went through the whole story of how I'd started the business, how I had helped grow it to over a million dollars in sales, and then how I came home one day and everything was gone.

You can imagine the shocked look on his face! Yet he was also impressed by what I'd done.

But I think he was even more surprised when I said, "I'm here today for one reason. *I'm here to ask you what did I do wrong?"*

So he thought for a moment, and then broke it all down for me. He told me everything I did right (which was a lot), and he also told me everything I did wrong. Still, that wasn't the most important part...

Because what I really got from that experience was the lesson that it's okay to ask for help and seek out advice. Also, it's important that we be acknowledged for the good that we do.

After such a heartbreaking experience, and after dusting myself off and then getting back on the horse -- to hear someone I respected simply acknowledge all that I had done right gave me hope.

I also realized just how obviously essential it was for me to turn pro in terms of making sure I always "CYA" legally in every business situation going forward. A true Sexy Boss business women would not trust just on a hand shake, she would get legal.

So in this instance, the reward I experienced were the lessons learned from jumping in and being on the business field with the big boys.

I knew, after this lesson I learned that I could go create the business again and build it with new information and experience...i.e. the Reward.

Stage 10: The Road Back

Stage ten is the road back to the ordinary world. So believe it or not, it's a stage. It's a stage of going back to what we think is our 'own' world. You've seen stories where people go back to their family or where they grew up. They go back to where they started to see not only how far they've come but to to return to the beginning and discover it in a new way.

For me, I went back to where it started in Texas, not as a place to hide but a place to rebuild. It was a place of foundation for me.

It could be internal -- maybe you revisit old beliefs or fears that you had before you started the journey and see them in new ways and to sweep them out and begin to rebuild.

If you have ever seen the movie *Citizen Kane* which was written and directed by Orson Wells -- Mr. Kane wants to go back to "Rose Bud". And in the very last scene the audience discovers what "Rose Bud" was. It was home. The entire story was about Mr. Kane's journey to the road back to his 'own' world.

What is your "Rose Bud"? How will you feel when you return?

Stage 11: The Resurrection Hero

This is where you cross the final threshold. You experience a resurrection and a transformation by your personal experience.

Eventually, I learned to put everything I discovered into action and began to go after something new and an idea that was bigger than me -- I also experienced the resurrection and the transformation to becoming a Sexy Boss. And then to spread the message.

I believe the resurrection is part of cleansing, letting go of people that might not serve you. It's new choices. It's maybe new romantic choices. It's kind of a catharsis, or a purging of the old. I believe that when you're on this hero's journey, there will be a time for death, there will be a time for purging.

There will be a time for what I call releasing, emotional releasing, or a profound emotional breakthrough; and this is where the resurrection, the transformation really becomes one of the most important pieces.

This is the stage where people might stop taking drugs if they are taking drugs; or they might get divorce, so they're done with the divorce, it's completed. They are maybe stepping into a new romantic relationship. If they stopped alcoholism, this is where they actually begin a new life after that.

They've already gone through the struggles of stopping being an alcoholic, stopping drinking. They've already gone through those struggles. Now they're like actually building something. They are experiencing the resurrection and the transformation. They're actually beginning to see their new life.

They're not what I call "caught in the aftermath" anymore. They really are creating a new life. That is a piece where many people don't go. They get caught in the swirl of the aftermath. They get their reward, and then they go back to the ordinary world, but they forget that there's a whole another level and a whole another energy.

Stage 12: Return With Elixir

This is where you return with the treasure to benefit the ordinary world. Let me say that in other terms. Being a sexy boss is returning with something special, bringing something to share with others.

This is where you continue the journey. It's a constant journey, but this is where you commence your new life, one that will be different forever because of the road you just traveled. And this is where are truly the hero, and you bring everything you learned to the forefront and actually share it with others.

For me, my treasure to the world, my elixir is being a Sexy Boss. This book is part of my new voice and how I help others create the life that they want. So they can own the power within themselves and be the architect of their reality.

Thoughts From a Sexy Boss

Going through your own unique hero's journey is imperative to becoming a Sexy Boss. It's how you grow, conquer your weaknesses and develop the presence to lead.

Being a Sexy Boss means leading yourself and others, everyday, no exceptions. And once you go through this process, passionate leadership becomes part of who you are.

Forget all the criticism, and forget about being nice. Be fierce and totally willing to disrupt any market or industry if you know you can do things better, and make a positive change as a Sexy Boss.

Chapter 10

Branding Yourself With Class

"A brand that captures your mind gains behavior. A brand that captures your heart gains commitment." -- Scott Talgo

A key step in the Sexy Boss process is turning yourself into a brand.

Because in business, being an entrepreneur, being in the new world -- ideas have become more important than ever.

Ideas are the beginning points of all fortunes. But let me clarify what I mean by ideas -- since there's a lot of misconceptions about that.

I'm not just talking about an idea for a new business -- I'm talking about the overall "big idea" that you use to package and promote yourself as a Sexy Boss.

That's a big difference. Even as an individual, even as an employee, you'll have so much more success if you can find an overriding idea that packages you well and helps others buy into who you are. And WHY they should be dealing with you.

The business and online worlds of today needs people who can create and promote ideas, including themselves. They don't need more employees or drones. They need ideas. People buy ideas. Companies buy ideas.

This ties into something I call, *"You, Inc."* -- because you are the idea. You have knowledge to sell; actually, it's your ideas and knowledge packaged in your own image and brand that must be sold.

Everyone Is a Brand, No Exceptions

So as a Sexy Boss who will have her own unique brand, it's your job to figure out what makes you unique and position yourself as a powerful brand.

Sure, many people just want to be drones. Let them! It's sad, but you can't save a drowning person until you yourself are safe. If you don't brand yourself, you'll be ignored in the world of business, and no matter how great your ideas are... they'll go unnoticed.

To be a Sexy Boss and thrive in today's society, you'll need to stand out and be remembered. You can't just blend in with the rest of the pack.

Think of those like Patti Stanger, star of the show *The Millionaire Matchmaker* -- with her Jewish New York "in your face" personality coupled with soft, caring heart. It's really unique and there's few others really like her. Certainly there's nobody else like her helping millionaires find love. So she stands out.

Another great example is Suze Orman. While I don't agree with her on everything, it's clear that she's built an amazing brand around herself that stands out and has gotten attention.

Was she always a successful author and TV host? Hell no! And that's my point -- like everyone, she had to begin building her brand early on. She honed her personality, what she stood for, what she focused on, how she could help people, until everything was clear and ready to stand out.

That's how she got attention and began to move up the ladder to greater levels of success and recognition. And it will be the same for you.

You must start branding yourself now!

How To Get Over Your Creative Blocks

Building the brand of who you are, what you stand for, and what you do takes real creativity at a level most people simply don't have.

Well, it's not that they don't "have" it -- we all do! It's that we're not used to accessing it.

A lot of people today don't feel they are creative. You hear the people say, "Oh, I'm not creative." I mean, I've had so many of my own friends say that!

And I smile and I think about that time when we were all in kindergarten and the teacher said, "Make a picture of a kitty cat," or "Make a picture of anything you want".

Because at that point, you never conceived of yourself as not being creative. You just expressed yourself without holding back. You painted, you wrote, you made things and they were all beautiful.

But as we grew up, we were judged and labeled by our peers -- maybe even laughed at. And most of us began to confine our creativity by bottling our own natural expressiveness, especially in terms of ideas and art. We "learned" the idea that we're not creative, it's not something we were born with.

The opposite is true -- we are all born as creative beings and each of us has our own creative strengths. It's come out, for instance, that I am not the most creative person when it comes to music.

When I was a kid, I played the flute, but I just had a hard time listening to all the different chords. I couldn't hear it. I didn't have that natural ability, and I didn't train myself for more than three or four years. I just gave up. I'm sure if I trained myself more, maybe I'd have a little more creativity in that area, but I just really didn't have a passion for it.

Why Creativity Takes Work

For me speaking in words, marketing and copywriting are more my creative strengths, and yet I still have to work at them. These are not things that come 100% naturally. Even the 100% natural athlete has to go to practice, or pick up the tennis racket, or swing the bat.

So just because you might be a natural at something, doesn't mean you don't have to pick up your pen and start writing -- pick up the guitar and start practicing.

It is challenging, but it is what drives riches and fortunes beyond your wildest dreams. And being a Sexy Boss, the *You, Inc.*, creativity is actually the natural state of your being.

My job in helping you be the Sexy Boss for yourself is to LIVE in that natural state of being where you're connected to your creative force and strengths, all the time.

That alone is not enough, though. You'll have to work at it. Every single day. You'll need to sit down and practice your creative endeavor, or think hard about how to creatively position the brand of You.

It's not something that will come to you overnight. You'll probably go down many roads that seemingly lead to nowhere. Until one day you have that big "aha" when everything comes together and you realize how to position yourself perfectly.

How to Not Let Others Destroy Your Creativity

Have you ever had an idea you were really excited about, told someone about it, and then they said, "That's stupid." Or some other negative remark. Or perhaps not that harsh, but they just analyzed it to death and picked it apart.

If so, you know what it feels like to have all your excitement and enthusiasm for an idea sucked out your body in an instant. It's a horrible feeling.

And that's why it's important to remember that criticism and judgment are often the enemies of the creativity process, especially in the early stages. Be sure that when you brainstorm or share your new ideas, it's done with other supportive, creative people. Not critics or analysts who will just knock the wind right out of your sails.

Don't give others the opportunity to bring you down.

Because ultimately, the wrong person may tell you an idea is stupid, or that they don't get your brand. Maybe you'll even feel rejected at times.

But it doesn't matter. View each of these challenges as a stepping stone to the success you'll ultimately have.

Know that as a Sexy Boss, no one can take away your creative power unless you let them. You alone have control over it.

This will build faith in who you are on a deep level, and allow you to be creative even in situations where you're the only one who believes in you, or your idea.

Show Me The Money!

There are people who create ideas, and there are people that put ideas into operation. Which one are you? Are you a creator or are you an organizer or are you an operator? The greatest fortunes are actually made by doing two things -- creating the idea and then helping put those ideas into action and operation.

There's a book I've read called, *One Simple Idea,* by Stephen Key. His profession is actually to sell his ideas to companies. He does not work for the company ever. He's not an employee of the company. He literally sells his ideas to the company and makes royalties.

The company then puts the idea into their system or overall operation, doing whatever is required -- whether it's a website or manufacturing or anything else. All he does for a living -- and trust me, he has a very, very plush lifestyle -- is literally comes up with ideas and sells them. He's like an inventor except he doesn't have to invent the actual thing.

This is the new way of our life. This is the new world. And he got this idea from an old toy called, *Teddy Ruxpin.*

The *Teddy Ruxpin* was a little bear and you put a cassette tape in back in the '80s, and the toy bear would actually teach the children something. It would talk to the children. And this was an idea that was created by a man, he sold the idea to a very large toy company and then he made royalties on that for many, many years. He did not manufacture it. He did not distribute it. He actually sold his idea to a large company and made a fortune.

There's a quote by Robert Kennedy. He is the former publisher of Muscle Magazine and many health magazines up until his death. He said…

> *"When you attach passion in your dream, you get yourself closer to achieving it." -Robert Kennedy (Publisher)*

And the reason I bring this up is because it's best to focus on ideas you are most passionate about. Because often times, you'll need to develop your idea or improve it or sell it, and if you're not passionate about it -- no matter how great it is -- you'll only get so far.

We Are Always Selling Ourselves, All The Time

When you become a Sexy Boss and you brand yourself, you understand that you are actually selling yourself all the time. When you're a politician, you sell yourself. When you're a lawyer, you sell yourself. When you're a customer service agent, you sell yourself. No matter what you're doing, you're selling yourself.

When I was actually 28 -- a little older in my career I guess -- is when I started to realize how I was not comfortable selling myself. My job was to get out in front of crowds and talk to them about real estate investing, how they should buy and sell real estate in this time of great prosperity in our country, and it wasn't easy or natural for me.

Because it wasn't just about real estate, I was selling them on why they should trust me. And that was really hard for me. So I actually decided to get out of the spotlight and work more on the business side and behind the scenes.

That was my way of stepping behind the curtain and not putting the spotlight on myself, because it scared me too much. It made me uncomfortable to think, "What if I fail? What will they think" Or "What if these people spend money and then they don't make any money in real estate, they're going to fault me!"

So I was scared. But that was 100% my issue and something I had to deal with.

My Journey Branding Myself

If I had known now what I knew then, I would have probably pushed through that fear sooner and made an effort to step into the spotlight at the age of 28. But since I was a woman, it was extremely easy for me to put myself in more of an assistant role and a supportive role to male speakers.

I was still being a Sexy Boss in other ways, helping run the business and grow the company and we were doing great. However, it's obvious now that I was running from an important experience that I needed to growth in.

It was easy to justify this decision, because that's what happened so often in this particular industry. The men would speak upfront and the woman would support and sell in the back.

However, I now realize that the decision to become a Sexy Boss means confronting these fears and being willing to disrupt what's "normal".

Why is this so important now? Because the process of branding yourself means being willing to step outside of the box and social norms and present yourself in a totally new, unique way.

This is not easy and it will take courage.

Virtue Versus Vanity

A Sexy Boss masters the distinctions between virtue and vanity.

Virtue can be a compelling force of good, however, in the case of me holding myself back for supposedly "good" reasons it was turned into a vice.

Similarly, pride can be a positive emotion -- however, it can also turn into vanity and hold you back. In my case, my vanity and fear of looking bad made me less willing to take a risk when it came to speaking.

Of course, there are different types of vanity. Women are allowed and even encouraged to be vain when it comes to their makeup or hair or another part of their physical appearance, but then that vanity and need to look good at all times can backfire on us.

On the other hand, men are allowed to be flashy with their watch or shoes, however, a man who looks in the mirror too much is considered vain in a very weak way. It's complicated!

But the biggest takeaway here is that as a woman, the need to be "perfect" and "look good" might be holding you back. You might be holding yourself back thinking about some virtue that isn't important.

Seriously. Some women tell themselves that it's better to not step into the spotlight because that makes them vain or an attention-whore, and those are undesirable qualities. Instead, they should be submissive and sit in the background.

Of course, we both know that's false.

The best course of action is what you truly feel called to do in your heart and by your higher self -- and that which helps the most people.

If you can help the most people behind the scenes and that's your calling great. But often, having the biggest impact means stepping up, walking to the front of the room (or stadium) and sharing what you know.

Cultivating Virtue in
The Sexy Boss Way Equals Courage

So being virtuous is really acquiring the courage to believe in yourself.

I believe in dharma, which is a Hindi word defined as something that supports life.

There's a quote by Mahama Barata, *"Dharma is the foundation that supports life."*

Dharma comes from the root word "dahar" which means "to support, uphold and nourish."

I believe we have control in how we are in certain situations, how we think, how we respond, and ultimately how we create within the situation.

Even in the case of an accident, something happens, you're driving down the street and then something totally out of your control happened. That is the reality. You could not control that. However, where you could have control is how you respond to the events that transpired.

Part of finding your dharma or calling is simply to listen to life.

For instance, when I was speaking in front of all those people about real estate investing, my dharma was being revealed to me. And yet, at the same time, I was unable to embrace that. I was unable to listen.

I couldn't hear it because I was too scared at the time. I see that now. But you can learn from my experience and use this process to recognize when dharma calls you and then listen.

This will influence everything you do, including the brand and key message you put forward about yourself.

Sexy Boss and Your Unique Brand Are Things You PRACTICE

Sexy Boss entrepreneurs are practitioners, first and foremost.

Being a Sexy Boss is a way of life, not a hobby. It's something that you do and practice every single day.

Your brand is a part of you, it should reflect who you are in deep and meaningful ways. It includes your passion, what you're doing, and everything you stand for.

For me, the Sexy Boss brand contains everything I'm about: Strength, Passion, Independence, Courage, Entrepreneurship, Sexiness, Perseverance, Positivity, Wealth, Abundance and so much more.

You may be undergoing the Sexy Boss process, but you'll be creating your own unique brand just as I have. And it will be something you practice.

That's a big lesson here, your brand should be built around who you are and what you practice every single day.

What are you willing to dedicate yourself to and practice out in the world every single day? What are you core values?

The women who are most successful in business have integrated their own person brand with their company. In fact, some of the ones we covered -- such as Suze Orman or Patti Stanger actually build their businesses as an extension of their own person brand.

Nothing More Powerful Than a Brand Whose Time Has Come

I want to go into a little bit about an idea that comes from an old biblical saying that says:

"Still other seeds fell on fertile soil, and they sprouted, grew, and produced a crop that was thirty, sixty, and even a hundred times as much as had been planted!"

When the big idea for branding yourself comes to you, it literally will come to you at the most random time -- maybe in the middle of night, or when you're driving, or while in the shower. It will just come to you. It won't be loud, but it will come to you.

When this bold idea for your brand is first planted in your mind, it must be treated very carefully. If not, you may forget it, or you may undervalue it and not take action.

The idea for your brand will begin as a powerful seed. And in time, as you develop and refine it, it will grow up into the sky and become powerful and immense.

There are many guides and programs out there for branding you. Some of them are valuable. However, the greatest value will come from you actively using this journey of self-discovery and all your creative faculties to think about your brand.

When you do that with discipline, consistency and practice -- it will eventually come to you in a flash. And then it's up to you to take that and develop the idea until it's ready to present to the world.

Final Thoughts from a Sexy Boss

We are all creative beings, and as a Sexy Boss, even more so. To realize your full potential and capacity for success, you'll need to turn your ideas into something tangible.

Brand both yourself and your ideas in order to get true visibility in the world. As a Sexy Boss making her way through a man's world, you may face more adversity in this process. But the rewards too will be greater.

Start branding yourself in everything you

Chapter 11

Building Your Business In A Man's World

"I had to make my own living and my own opportunity. But I made it! Don't sit down and wait for the opportunities to come. Get up and make them." -- Madame C.J. Walker, first female millionaire entrepreneur

Life is short. Creating a Sexy Boss business that empowers you and others is the single best way to help realize all your dreams.

Up until today, things haven't always been equal for men and women. In many professions, women unfortunately still don't get equal pay for the same job.

The good news is that with the rise of the Internet and the plethora of marketing tools available, you can build your business and beat men at their own game.

Yes, armed with what you're about to discover, you will be in complete control of your own destiny. You can create unlimited wealth, and it will all be yours.

Yes you!

But unlocking your own personal river of money begins with something you might not yet understand...

Everyone Is In The Internet Marketing Business

Nowadays, virtually everyone is on the Internet. Even many mom and pop stores have begun to create an Internet presence. Especially now with smart phones, everyone is connected to the Internet all the time.

And that means you're at an incredibly severe handicap if you don't have a solid website and online marketing plan.

- People must be able to search for your business and find you
- They must be able to check out your website and learn more about you
- They should be able to read real reviews of your website or product on someplace like Yelp or Amazon or another site
- And they must feel that they can trust doing business with you

I speak for most people in the modern world when I say that if a company doesn't have a website or any reviews that I can find, I usually won't deal with them. It's just a fact.

We live in a different time. Not having a website or online presence doesn't just make you hard to trust -- it makes your business invisible!

Why Internet Marketing Is <u>THE</u> Most Important Modern Skill

If you want to build your business in a man's world, you'll need to know the fastest, most effective ways to grow it. Period.

While there are many, many aspects of running a successful online business -- marketing can be broken down into a few different categories.

1) Traffic. This is how you get visitors to your site, or to your physical business, if you own an actual store. You might get traffic from Google search, from Facebook ads, from a variety of places. But it's all traffic.
2) Conversion. Once somebody comes to your site, you want them to take action. Whether it's joining your list, buying your product or visiting your store, you'll need a clear, measurable strategy for making sure you "convert" a visitor into a lead or a customer.

3) Relationship. Once you have leads and customers that are tied to your business, you'll need ongoing strategies that keep you in touch with them and help you sell more things to them. This could include email, social media, a smart phone app and more.

Overall, the process of Internet marketing boils down to those three steps. Traffic gets people to your site... conversion turns them into customers... then your ongoing relationship with them determines how valuable they'll be to your business over time.

In reality, it gets more complicated because there are so many things you can do in each of those areas -- from search engine optimization, to tracking and analytics -- but the point I want you to see is how this overall process works.

Now, let's look at how it can make you rich.

Marketing = Growth = Money

Let's say that you've got an idea for a business -- you want to sell gluten free desert information, recipes and instruction. Let's call you the "Gluten Free Desert Girl" -- that's the name of your business. It's not perfect, but it's good enough for now...

So now, you create your cookbook, which you sell for $10. You launch your website, and initially the sales are slow. You tell some friends, get your site listed on search engines, create a Facebook page, and so on.

Initially you get 200 visitors to your site each week. 5% of those visitors actually buy your book, which is great.

And that means you're making 10 sales per week.

10 sales x $10 = $100/week

That's $400 per month and $4800 per year.

Not a bad start!

Next, you use one of the many traffic techniques available to increase the number of visitors to your site. It could be that you have your site optimized for search traffic (this is called "Search Engine Optimization or SEO")... or you get your site listed on a popular review site someplace with high visibility.

This doubles the number of people coming to your site each week, which also doubles your sales to 20 each week.

Now, you're making $800/month and $9600 per year.

Getting better!

Next, you hire a pro copywriter and he changes the words on your page that sell your cookbook, and this doubles the "conversion" -- which in this case, is the number of people who buy your book.

Now 10% of the people who land on your site buy your cookbook. That means that you're now selling 40 books each week -- this is $1600 per month and $19,200 each year.

Imagine that you create a Gluten-Free Desert DVD, and you begin selling this to anyone who has purchased your book. It sells for $20 and 20% of your customers end up buying it when you email them about it.

If you we're selling 40 books each week, that's 160 new customers each month. If 1/4 of them buy your DVD, that's 40 DVD customers and $800 in extra revenue each month.

All of the sudden, your business is doing $2400 each month with very little cost.

Now, you're making $2400/month and $28,000 per year.

Why The Internet Gives You The Ultimate Leverage

Now, my fellow Sexy Boss -- this is where it gets really fun.

Imagine at this point that you increase your number of visitors by placing free teaser videos on Youtube with links back to your site. Simple, right?

And this doubles your traffic yet again. Suddenly, you're getting 800 visitors each week and your little business is selling $4800 worth of products each month. That's probably almost enough to quit your job!

Even if not, don't worry, because I'm sure by now you see the potential.

Once you have something that's working, you just need to generate more traffic, add more products, enhance your overall sales and marketing process and the sky is the limit.

Even a Sexy Boss business focused on teaching Gluten-Free Desert making could do a million dollars or more each year with the right traffic and product strategies.

And that's amazing -- only on the Internet can you launch a business very little cost or risk, yet still have the potential to be big and give you the freedom you've always wanted.

How do you know what business you should be in?

Passion + Expertise + Market Size

There are several key criteria that will help you determine how to create and build your Sexy Boss business. Ignore any one of these and you'll limit yourself, if not fail outright.

On the other hand, if you nail each one, you'll have laid the foundation for a seven-figure business.

Here they are:

1) Passion. This is the first and most obvious one. But you'd be shocked by how many people overlook this. Why? Greed, usually. However, not focusing your business around something you're passionate about is one of the dumbest things you could ever do.

First of all, because you won't enjoy what you do each day. At best, you'll feel lukewarm about it. And at worst, you'll hate what you're doing. In that case, you might as well have a job! Seriously.

So be sure that whatever idea you choose to build your business around, it's something you're deeply passionate and enthusiastic about. That's the only way you're going to be willing to push through all the challenges of growing a successful company long after the initial excitement wears off. (And it will wear off).

2) Expertise. Make sure you pick an area where you can be an expert. Sometimes you already are an expert in a certain area -- and you're also passionate about that subject -- so the choice is easy.

But maybe you're coming from a job and you're not an expert in any area that you'd love to dedicate your life to, in terms of building a business. That's okay.

However, it's wise to select an area where you at least CAN be an expert. To use our earlier example, you could become an expert in the area of gluten-free deserts, if that's your passion. There aren't many experts in that area, so it would be easier to stand out and make a dent. Or it could be anything you're interested in or passionate about. As long as it meets the third and final criteria...

3) Market size. This is just as important as the previous two, because it determines how big your business can really be. Remember, you could be passionate about blueberry pudding, and you could very well be the world's leading expert on blueberry pudding -- but can you build a million-dollar business around that?

Probably not. It's too narrow of a topic and thus a very small market. Better if you choose an area that has at least somewhat broader appeal, so that you can reach more people and have a bigger, more successful company.

I'm not saying you need to shoot for something ultra-mass market either -- being too broad is another problem. But find the happy medium.

One simple way is to run a Google search for key words around your topic and see how many searches there are. All combined, there should be millions of searches for your topic. Also, there should be multiple businesses that have at least six-figure annual sales, or larger.

Even if you'd have multiple competitors with millions in sales, that's great. Don't worry about competition right now, at least it shows there's money to be made in that market and you know it's a subject you're passionate about.

Once you've discovered something you want to pursue as the centerpiece of your business, let's look at an overview of starting an online business.

The Online Success Blueprint

To build a Sexy Boss business that gives you maximum freedom, you'll need to understand everything that's required in order to make it succeed online.

So let's quickly overview some of the steps you'll need to take:

Vision and Goal-Setting. Why are you doing this? What's the overriding purpose? What freedom are you creating? And that freedom is a choice. And then what's the clarity? What's the main objective?

Get really clear on on exactly WHY you're starting the business.

Market Research and Selection. We touched on this already. It's imperative that you look at your market and know you can build a viable company in that area. Some of the most popular and lucrative niches are health, finance, fitness, dating, entertainment, fashion, and pets, just to name a few.

Planning. This is the overall planning of the actual business. From the name to the actual programs you use to run and manage your business, it's all vital.

Software and systems are a key piece of any business, especially online. You'll need to know the particular software systems that work well in information online marketing businesses.

Internet Marketing Techniques. There are countless Internet marketing techniques and strategies out there, from traffic and social media... to copywriting and conversion. Many topics have entire courses dedicated to just that one thing.

This is not to intimidate you, just to let you know that it would be impossible to cover those techniques in a book like this.

Right now, it's just important to keep in mind that the techniques and strategies you'll learn nearly always fall into one of the three categories we discussed earlier -- traffic, conversion, and relationship.

Company Formation and Legalities. You'll need to know how to create your company in the US, what kind of company to create, the terms and agreements or terms of service on the website, and more.

Remember, you are creating a real company that's going to create a real product or service, and you want to make sure you go pro, not amateur. All your ducks must be in a row.

Creating Your Systems. The beauty of an online business is that it can run automatically and make you money while you sleep. But that doesn't happen by accident. It's something you set up and create, by thinking wisely about the systems that will work behind the scene -- from sales, to payment processing, support, customer service and more.

Product Creation. Once you know the topic you'll be building your business around, you'll need to create your product or products. In information marketing, there's different things you can create all by doing online things. So here we go into product creation and that could be: audio, writing, video, transcription, coaching, e-books, books on Amazon which is different than e-books, membership sites, e-commerce sites, and more.

Numbers and analytics. When you own a business and you're a pro at business, you understand the numbers. You know how much traffic you're getting, what your conversion is, the lifetime value of your customers, the efficiency of your sales funnel, your refund rate and countless other metrics. Many programs will do most of this for you, so don't worry -- it's not necessary that you figure it all out. You just need to learn how to use the appropriate tools.

Outsourcing. Outsourcing is going to be a critical piece depending on how you want to build your business. Do you want to build your business where you have five employees that go to job every day or do you want to have virtual business where you manage and work with others from a distance?

With outsourcing, it's possible to lower your overhead costs and build a more "lean" and profitable company. But only if you know how to do it intelligently.

As you grow and are profitable, you can choose to add in-house employees later on as needed to help you take your company to the next level. But it's not always necessary. A friend of mine has a $20 million+ business in the dating niche that is all virtual -- nobody works with him in his office. And it does amazing.

How All The Pieces Fit Together

I hope you see two things here. First, that starting an online business around something you love -- in an area with the potential to make you rich -- is one of the smartest things you could ever do.

Note: It's also one of the *craziest* things you could ever do, because it takes a ton of thought and work in order to get it right. It's not something that you build overnight, despite what any late night infomercial tells you.

It will test you and demand that you grow as a business woman and Sexy Boss -- so get ready.

The good news is that there's never been a better time to do this. There are more tools than ever before for starting, growing and automating an online business -- and more and more women are launching kickass, million-dollar businesses right out of their home.

If they can do it, you can too. Even if the thought is intimidating to you right now, that's a good thing.
That means you'll be stretched and you'll grow in the process of creating your own Sexy Boss business that gives you the wealth and freedom you know you deserve.

Final Thoughts From A Sexy Boss

As a Sexy Boss, wealth is important mostly because it gives you more freedom. Still, the greatest freedom of all will come from owning your own successful online business – which gives you both money and freedom.

Your highest leverage comes from using Internet Marketing to launch your Sexy Boss business, and continually grow it until you're swimming in a river of money.

Yes, it will be challenging. But there's also never been a better time to get started. And there's no excuses, because unlike many other fields, this is a 100% level playing field. You can do it!

Get started in thinking about and building your Sexy Boss business, today.

Chapter 12

Grow Faster By Finding Your Robin

"Finding each other is the beginning, staying together is the process, working together is the success." -- Maeagn Gunderson

No Sexy Boss ever succeeds alone. It's a team effort.

And therefore, you'll need to actively build your team early on.

I call this "finding your Robin" and it's more than just your business team -- it's everyone who supports you in your path.

For example, my Robin is more than one person. It's my lovely dog, Lady... my project manager... my significant other... it's my friends... it's my business coach – because each and every one of them protect me, save me, and ultimately push me to go to the next level to be great.

Remember: Robin saved Batman's life many times. Robin sometimes is more significant than Batman.

Without Robin, Batman wouldn't have caught as many criminals, and there are many times when he might have been dead had it not been for Robin's help.

It's the same for me. There are times I would have totally failed if not for my team -- they've helped me in countless ways, in a variety of key moments.

And your team will do the same for you.

Forget the Fairy Tale, Build Your Team

And if you look at Disney, we were taught as little girls as princesses to be saved by the prince. The underlying message is that that we cannot help ourselves and we must be saved.

The princess always needs the prince to come along and rescue her -- without him she is helplessly trapped in the tower, or castle.

However in the real world that's not the case. Not as Sexy Boss at least!

Being a Sexy Boss, you're in the Batman position. You're the leader and the super hero, you're the one making things happen. You're not waiting to be rescued.

And that means you'll need to find your Robin, but not out of desperation or the need to be saved, but from a place of strength. From the knowledge and conviction that -- while you can do a lot yourself -- you can do more with the help and support of others who are aligned to your vision.

Yes, you choose to be the Batman, and like Batman, you go and help others. But you always have a Robin; you always have people in your life – coaches, mentors, family, and friends who support you and help lift you up.

So, the question I have for you is *"Who is your Robin?"*

The World's Most Powerful Individuals Always Have Teams Around Them

Don't try to be a Lone Ranger in business, it won't work. In our last chapter, we covered a lot and still we barely scratched the surface of what it takes to build and grow a successful online business. There's absolutely no way you can handle everything -- from product creation to web development, traffic, customer support, finances and more. It's impossible!

Even the best writers and consultants often have teams! So start with what part you're best at, be clear on what you're good at, and then build a team that helps fill in your weaknesses or gaps.

And you might have to learn new skills. You might have to learn copywriting. You might have to learn more about Internet marketing. But again, you can't learn and do everything. You'll have to rely on others for assistance.

One thing I find interesting is that the world's most successful CEO's often have the biggest support teams around them. Not just assistants, but managers, financial experts, vice presidents, and so on.

We've talked about Steve Jobs and Bill Gates in previous chapters -- two of the most successful business leaders in history. Well, both relied heavily upon their Robin -- their team that supported and reported to them every single day. Without the right team in place, they wouldn't have accomplished even a tiny fraction of what they ultimately did. And it will be the same for you.

Find a Mentor -- Fast!

Building on the fact that you cannot do it alone, know that you'll ideally need to find a mentor who's been where you are. Someone who has built a business in the way you are trying to build yours.

Everyone has mentors -- yes, everyone!

Ideally, your mentor has built a business himself or herself, so he or she can truly help you navigate the waters when the going gets tough.

Be sure to ask the question: "Have you built a successful business?" Or "Have you done this {project} successfully at least once?" If not, they may still be able to help you, but I'm a firm believer that at least one of your mentors should be someone who has actually built a business. This helps you in countless ways.

Also, be careful of people who claim that they are the way, the truth, and you don't need to go anywhere else in life. Those individuals are dangerous!

Nobody has all the knowledge, especially when it comes to online business. Because so much of it is literally changing every single month. There are principles that stay the same as you grow the business -- many of them we covered in the last chapter, like traffic or conversion.

However, the specific techniques -- like how to rank high on a search engine -- those things change all the time and there's no one rule or technique that lasts forever.

So nobody can know everything all the time, be weary of anyone saying that.

Forget Easy, Get Ready to Fail Your Way to Success

"People fail forward to success." Mary Kay Ash

The beauty of finding your Robin is that you can personally fail and they'll be there to help you get back up and stay on the path to success.

I have personally fallen, I have skinned my knees, I bruised my toes, stumbled into all the roadblocks, and gone through virtually every type of "test" out there.

173

I have been down the road. Choosing to be the Sexy Boss in your life, choosing to be the CEO of your life, is not the easiest path.

An easier path is the following: It's going through your life depending on others, being trapped in the job, being told what to do, to showing up at 9:00, leaving at 5:00, not caring what happens in between, getting the paycheck on time, and paying your bills on time.

That's absolute torture for the Sexy Boss inside of you, but it's also easier in many ways than challenging and pushing yourself.

Living your life as being the 100% responsible of your life is a Sexy Boss. But that does not mean you have to do it all alone. Having a team you can trust and rely on means you can be bold and take risks, knowing they'll be there to help you and support you through the process.

And vice versa, you'll do the same for them. Batman also saved Robin's life many times as well. It's a symbiotic relationship.

My close friend Joe Sugarman -- who has built many successful businesses, including the BluBlocker line of sunglasses -- said he became successful precisely because he failed more times than he succeeded.

Having the right team around you helps give you the confidence to "fail forward" -- knowing that each little setback or failure brings you one step closer to success.

More Adversity Usually Means More Money and Success

Another great part about having the right team is that it allows you to take on bigger challenges with more adversity. Because the greater the adversity, the greater the reward.

Remember, as a Sexy Boss, your skin is going to grow thick and your heart might feel like it's going black.

But I promise you through the journey that you'll learn that having thick skin is quite fun and having a tough heart gives you the power to extremely give your love and your power more powerfully to your cause, to your family, your team, and to build your business greater than ever before.

If you just have this open, soft heart all the time, it is a place where people can grab and take. The "black heart" doesn't mean that you protect your heart or avoid risks. The opposite, in fact. It's that you give your heart a 100,000% to what you choose to give it to, and no one can take your power or push you around. People can no longer take your energy.

You choose to give, and you choose to give powerfully. Especially to your team. You really give your whole heart to your team, because they are the one going into battle with you every single day.

Think about it like this: With the right team in place, you can set a more ambitious goal for your business. Maybe it's to build a ten million dollar company rather than a one million dollar one. Great!

Because there will be greater challenges and adversity in attempting to go to that higher place, but with the right heart and the right team, you'll be able to get there.

Still, this begets the question: "How do you know who is right to be on your team?"

Well, fortunately I've uncovered some core traits of the Sexy Boss that you can use as criteria for selecting who will be a good fit to work with you.

Use this list as a tool for evaluating prospective members of your team.

The 12 Core Traits of a
Sexy Boss (And Her Team-mates!)

To be a Sexy Boss, or work at a high level with a Sexy Boss, members of your team should have most (or ideally all!) of these things in order. Or at least, to aspire to these various traits.

Here they are:

1. Positive mental focus. Does this person focus on what they want? Are they clear about what they want? When things get tough, does their mind go positive and focus on solutions -- or negative and focus on problems?

2. Personal top health. Yes, health is important for you and your team. Building a Sexy Boss business requires energy, and having energy requires good health. You ideally want team members who respect their own body, how they feel, and want to live a balanced, healthy lifestyle.

3. Strong human relationships. The best team members are those who already have strong relationships with others. So check and see if the person you're considering has mentors, or quality friendships, or other meaningful relationships. Remember, it's about quality not quantity!

4. Freedom from fear. You want people with courage and willingness to take risks. Otherwise, they'll never be able to support you. Remember, building a Sexy Boss business is inherently risky -- you need those who understand this and have the balls to put themselves on the line with you every single day.

5. A clear mental mindset of a future achievement. Does this person know where he or she wants to be? Is he or she clear on her goals? You want someone with a strong future-orientation because that's what will help you move the business forward, rather than be fixated on the past.

6. Confidence in crisis situations. How does your potential team member handle stress or crisis? Can this person be calm, poised and decisive? This is vital as you can't build a team around everyone freaking out the moment things get chaotic. Because every business does get that way at some point.

7. An attitude of gratitude. The last thing you need is a Negative Nancy or a Debbie Downer on your team! Choose people who are grateful for all that they have, and who are focused on making a positive contribution in the lives of others. A Sexy Boss business is ultimately in business to serve and enrich the lives of its customers. And that can only happen when all members of the team are aligned to that reality.

8. Healthy romantic relationships. Granted, not everyone is a relationship -- I'm not saying you should only hire people who are happily married or in a committed relationship. The point is, this person cares about being in a healthy, romantic, supportive relationship -- just like you do. You don't want someone who is in an abusive, up and down, roller coaster type relationship that affects their state of mind or performance as a team member.

9. Open mind to all people. This one is obvious, but it's very important that anyone on your team be accepting and supportive of everyone else -- regardless of age, sex, ethnicity, sexual orientation or anything else. That's the only way you'll have a fully positive environment... even if you work remotely and away from your team.

10. Full self-discipline. Does this person take care of themselves? Are they well put together? Do they take care of their body and health? Do they update their business skills regularly? Do they show up on time? Do they not waste time while working? All these things come down to self-discipline and it's important to screen for this early on.

11. People wisdom. Ideally, you want team members who are not only intelligent -- but emotionally intelligent. Meaning they understand people on a deeper level. This will help your team overall to make better decisions about customers or directions the business should take.

12. The Desire for Personal Financial Wealth. Yes, you also want members of your team to want wealth -- because they'll be more motivated to succeed and take the business higher. Those who don't care about money or wealth will just see working with you as "job" that gets them by, and not have the same passion or drive as someone who truly wants to take part in the success that's created by your Sexy Boss business.

Does every member of your team need to have every single one of these qualities? No, but the more they have, the better.

And at worst, they should aspire to all of these things -- so that they are internally aligned with you and what you stand for as a Sexy Boss.

This will not only help you make smart decisions about who you choose to be on your team, but also knowing they have these qualities, you'll be able to trust them so much more.

Because they are like you, and they will be able to support you -- and you to them.

Just like Batman and Robin.

Final Thoughts from a Sexy Boss

No greatness was ever achieved in total isolation. Every great player had coaches and teammates who helped him. Every great leader had a strong support network of people.

Fulfilling your potential as a Sexy Boss requires building a team of individuals around you who are aligned with your vision and ready to go to battle on your behalf.

Use the 12 Core Traits of a Sexy Boss to assist you in building a powerful team that you can rely on and trust.

Chapter 13

Many Minds Are Better Than One

"I've always believed that one woman's success can only help another woman's success." - Gloria Vanderbuilt, Artist and Actor

This final chapter is all about the power of the mastermind.

But first, what is power?

I believe power is essential for success and accumulation of money, but I want to actually define it.

And I'm going to define it word for word from the book, *Think and Grow Rich* by Napoleon Hill.

According to him, *power can be defined as "organized and intelligently directed acknowledge."*

Power, as the term is used here, refers to organized effort sufficient to enable an individual to transmute desire into its monetary equivalent. Organized effort is produced in the coordinated effort of two or more people who work towards a definite end in a spirit of harmony.

Power is required for the accumulation of money. Power is necessary for the retention of money after it has been accumulated. That is power.

And so today we are going to talk about the mastermind alliance, and how power can aid you as a Sexy Boss entrepreneur.

Harnessing Energy You Don't See

What is energy?
Well, energy is the nature's universal set of building blocks -- it's that which constructs every material thing in the universe.

You may or may not have heard the expression, "thoughts are things"... because it's based on the notion that thoughts are actual energy. Thus, there are material consequences to how and what you think at each moment.

There is a man named Neil Donald Walsh whose philosophy that everything has already been here, and it's just up to us as human beings to tap into that which has existed and turn that energy into a manifestation of reality. I believe that too.

And in the world of energy, these building blocks are available to you and to me no matter where you are in the world.

I know this sounds far out, but one way to think about this is the thoughts you have about your business -- well those are building blocks. The more of those little positive building blocks you accumulate and then make real through action, the more your business becomes reality.

And this is true for any dream, and for any person on this earth.

It's not about where you're from, what nationality you are, your sex or age or appearance. This energy is total impartial and accessible by all human beings.

Yes -- this is available to every human being here on this Earth.

Your Brain, The World's Most Powerful Battery

We all have experience with flashlights or things that run on batteries -- toys, kid toys, or cameras -- and we notice that when we put one battery in there, it will create a certain amount of power.

However, when we put more than one battery in there, it's not one plus one equals two. It is actually more like one plus one equals ten. And the more energy and the more battery juice that you have that goes into something, the more that thing has.

And so group of brains are like batteries in that the whole is greater than the sum of its parts. Put multiple minds together and they'll emerge and be greater than the individual minds could ever just be on their own.

You've probably had this experience. Maybe you had a problem or something you were pondering and felt stuck.

And so you spoke to someone about it. Could just be a simple conversation. But the moment you put two minds on that problem or topic, something changes. More power is accessed than your mind, or that person's mind.

It's almost as though a new mind is created between the two of you.

And I bring this up because we've all had that experience, talked about the issue with someone else, and then had that "aha" about the answer or solution. It's probably happened to you more times than you can count.

The Mastermind Begins to Help You Connect This Power

The mastermind is literally the gathering of many minds. Quite often, mastermind groups meet and focus on a particular topic. It could be marketing, or writing, or science, or anything.

The important thing is that people are coming together in an open space to share and expand their individual minds.

One thing I've discovered, and why I put this chapter last, is that mastermind groups tend to be used more by those who are more advanced in business.

Ironic that those who are more advanced actually seek out more help and collaboration with others -- but it makes perfect sense. To succeed at progressively higher levels, it's imperative to shed your ego.

Once you do this, you become more and more open to the thoughts and contributions of others who might have a different perspective or knowledge base than the one you have.

Using "Other Knowledge" To Speed Your Success

What is "other knowledge"?

I believe that when you have multiple people together in one place, all in spirit of harmony going towards a specific goal or helping each other out in each specific goal, you're accessing a different type of knowledge.

First, there's book knowledge, the kind you can walk into the library and get or buy a book and purchase.

There's also the second type called, the knowledge of personal experience. This is something that has been accumulated over a period of time.

We all have this in some way. For me, after many businesses that I've created and failed, I have experiential knowledge in this area. It can be highly specific too: For instance, the real estate boom and bust that I personally went through, that experiential knowledge that came from what I lived through.

And then there is a third type of knowledge, the wisdom of infinite intelligence knowledge. This is one of the key powers of the mastermind where you have four individuals, four brains that are in touch with all three of those different kinds of knowledge.

They have their personal knowledge, the knowledge they have read, as well as their connection with the infinite intelligence.

Infinite intelligence is often the most powerful because it can help you uncover answers that normal reasoning or experience can't help. Infinite intelligence is creative. It's about tapping into solutions that can't usually be seen.

How the Sexy Boss Gets (and Gives) Even More Power Via a Mastermind

So how do you as a Sexy Boss entrepreneur use the mastermind to actually create something tangible? Well, you actually begin by creating and having an experience with an actual mastermind group.

A mastermind is again two or more people in coming together, sharing their knowledge and desired wisdom in harmony. This could be your spouse. This could be your significant other. It could be your mother, or your father. It could be your best friend!

As long as there are multiple brains, as long as there are two or more individuals coming together in a conversation where they are co-creating -- that qualifies as a mastermind.

There are different ways you can structure a mastermind. You can buy into a mastermind. I've been part of marketing masterminds that are fairly expensive, yet also priceless in terms of the expertise and knowledge available.

You can also just bring colleagues, friends or family together in a mastermind. Paid or unpaid, experts or not, the main point is having multiple minds coming together, working in harmony.

Remember what we discussed last chapter about finding your Robin and building your team? Well, in a perfect world, your team is also an amazing mastermind group. In the sense that you regularly come together, work and share in harmony, and that the sum of your minds is greater than the individual parts.

Your Ego May Resist At First, But Once You Try It...

As women, we usually want to support other people. But allowing other people, in the case of a mastermind group, to support us in our growth and development is usually a new shift for us.

But that is how we multiply our energy. I want to make sure you understand that.

This is why it can also be helpful and even crucial to be part of mastermind groups that are dedicated to sharing and supporting you as a Sexy Boss entrepreneur -- and not just the team you work with.

Because not every group is a mastermind, just as not every group exists to support you in the growth of your business or personal success. You might have a spouse that's not in your mastermind.

This is because, again, the power of the mastermind comes from two or more brains uniting in *spirit of harmony* towards a specific mission or goal. That is often not a key trait of many relationships or friendships, so keep that distinction in mind.

How to Get 150 Years of Experience Overnight

I remember being part of a mastermind group and someone remarked that it had 150 years of experience behind it. And I thought to myself, *"150 years of experience?"*

I'm looking at the individuals in the room, and they're in their 30s and 40s and I'm thinking "What? This doesn't make any sense."

But if you take each person and each person, has 15 years of experience in that specific industry and there's 10 people, that's 15 times 10. Which comes out to 150 years of experience. And that really is a massive multiplication of energy and power.

Notice that I have only talked about addition, and haven't said anything about competition. And that's because competition is not at all part of the mastermind experience.

One of sillier things I hear from other entrepreneurs as well as my clients and customers is *"Well, I don't want to tell anybody about my idea. Someone might steal it,"* or *"I don't want to share my secrets. Someone might take them,"* whatever it is.

Please understand, going back to these three types of knowledge, A, B and C -- (A) book knowledge; (B) personal experience; and (C) infinite intelligence.

In the case of all big ideas, they come from a place of infinite intelligence. They are part of a subconscious reality as Carl Jung described, one that we're all connected to.

In reality, your idea is already out there, and it's not your secret to hold on. It's your job to use it, to execute on that insight or understanding that you've been given -- which every great genius or inventor has done throughout history.

Clinging to your idea with a sense of fear or limitation is often a sure way that nothing happens with it -- or worse, that you encourage others to take it from you because you are guarding it rather than focusing on turning it into reality.

Letting Go Of The Limited, Competitive Mind

So when I hear people say, "Oh, I don't want to share," I look at that person and say they are from a competitive mind, not a cooperative mind.

Of course, I'm not saying there is no such thing as intellectual property. I'm practical. Sure, there are times when you have to seal your ideas for a certain period of time, while you trademark or patent them, that's fine.

Just know that it's in the sharing of ideas that the real power comes from.

I know this from experience. I've always been a very competitive person. That has served me in many ways in life. In business, it served me, but it's also just destroyed me in many ways when I've come into a situation where people wanted to collaborate and share.

And rather than share, I was overly competitive -- which put others on edge and lowered the overall trust within the group.

I see that now, especially as a young girl in my early 20's in corporate America, I became very competitive and rose up the ladder. That competitive spirit fueled and drove me to succeed.

But few months after I had rise to the top, I was basically forced out because I was not in a place where I wanted to help the team or help the company. I was just really in it for myself, I didn't care about anyone else, and they knew that.

And so it eventually led to some painful falls while I was younger in business.

Share and Self-Promote Without Being Boastful

As you ponder what we just discussed, it's important you understand the difference between self-promotion versus competition.

Often when a person you come across is being boastful, you'll find a person who is secretly doubtful and afraid.

But being boastful is different than self-promotion. I look at Oprah and Donald Trump and even George Clooney and the famous actresses like Angelina Jolie who are very good at self-promotion -- that doesn't mean they're boastful.

That's something that I had to really had to learn on my own. I was taught by one of my parents that being a star is a bad thing. *"How dare they ask for the spotlight. Those are boastful, selfish people."*

They even told me that that they didn't like Oprah, and I believed this for years. And what I've learned is that Oprah and Donald Trump and people of that nature are amazing self-promoters. By promoting themselves and what they stand for, they actually help thousands and millions of people around the world to be their best. Nothing wrong with that!

Just look at Dr. Phil. Oprah actually helped make Dr. Phil famous. The same with Dr. Oz. Trump has helped others become famous and successful as well.

Promoting yourself with confidence is not the same thing as being competitive. It's about sharing who you are and what you stand for.

And it's possible to do this in an open, humble way that actually serves the higher goals and vision of the mastermind group.

Thinking In Infinite Terms

I believe that one of the principles that most amazing entrepreneurs have is that they think infinite versus finite. Let me explain what thinking infinite versus finite means.

Entrepreneurs that become rich and keep that wealth don't think in terms of limitations. They don't have a "scarcity mindset" and think, "If I make money in this market, others will be making less."

This is important, because it can be immensely valuable if you have a mastermind group within your specific industry. I personally am involved in mastermind groups where you'd think the people in the group are competitors.

In reality, they do have competing businesses -- but at the same time, all these entrepreneurs realize that their success does not take away from the other person. So they share openly. You'd be shocked at all the "business secrets" they just let their "competitors" know about.

Again, it's about thinking in infinite terms, rather than scarcity. When you do that, you realize that you can grow and grow and just because others make more money -- it doesn't mean there's less for you.
So being the Sexy Boss, it's important that you help other entrepreneurs, and they will help you in return. You picking up the phone saying, "Hey, I need help on this. What do you

think of this idea?" That will happen to you, and they'll say, "Hey, I have an idea for you."

I've had people send me books, send me articles, send me things and go, "Hey, I thought of you. I thought of you when I read this article. Here's an article that might serve you in your business." That's amazing!
I will give back to that person tenfold. Why? Because that's how entrepreneurs are. The entrepreneurial spirit is not about hoarding, it's about creating, growing, expanding. Be really clear on that.

5 Steps To Creating Your Mastermind

Let's finish this chapter on a practical note. How do you go about creating a mastermind? What are the steps?

1) Find others who want to come together to share and collaborate. This is rule number one. Because if the spirit of the mastermind group is not right -- if there's not a collective energy of support, sharing, and collaboration for a greater good -- it will fail.

2) Find others with experience that compliments your own. This could be people with different businesses in your niche or industry who see things with different eyes, or who've had a different set of challenges than you have.

Or it could be bringing people together from totally different industries with radically different skills and perspectives. If you follow the first step and the spirit of the group is right, either choice you make in step 2 will be fine.

3) Make sure there is commitment and consistency. Yes, doing just one mastermind is valuable. However, meeting regularly will allow you to connect and build deeper relationships with the people in your group. As the connection between the group grows, trust is enhanced and there's more potential for progress.

4) Make sure the environment is open and distraction-free. Don't come together in a place where people are going to be afraid of opening up or discussing their business or the issue at hand. For example, if your mastermind is about teaching dating advice -- some members of the group might not want to discuss that around people who don't understand the business.

Also, holding your mastermind in an area where outside people can overhear or distract you is not a good idea. Many mastermind groups are held in private conference rooms or work spaces for this reason. It gives the group privacy and the freedom to share freely.

5) Lastly, be honest with everyone and make sure they give 100%. A mastermind only works if everyone is fully engaged, wants to be there and is giving 100%. If you sense that someone is holding back or not fully participating, don't be afraid to give them your honest feedback. You don't have to do it harshly or as criticism.

The point of the mastermind is participation, support and the group being greater than the sum individual parts. For that to happen, everyone has to be fully present and dedicated to sharing.
That's when the magic happens. That's when you'll experience the unparalleled power of the mastermind group, and how it helps you take your Sexy Boss business to new heights.

Final Thoughts From A Sexy Boss

Many minds are more powerful than one. Creating or joining a Mastermind allows you to tap into a higher intelligence, many more years of experience, and achieve success faster.

It may take your ego a moment to acknowledge its potency or necessity, but once you see what's possible for you via a strong, open Mastermind group – there's no going back.

Use the steps outlined at the end of this chapter to create the ultimate mastermind group, one that supports and helps expand both you and your Sexy Boss business!

Be You. Be Real. Be Sexy Boss!

Because...

Being the Boss is Sexy!

About The Author

Heather Ann Havenwood, CEO of Havenwood Worldwide, LLC and Chief Sexy Boss, is a serial entrepreneur and is regarded as a top authority on internet marketing, business strategies and marketing.

Since marketing her first online business in 1999, bringing together clients and personal coaches, she has played an active role in the online marketing world since before most even had a home computer.

In 2006 she started, developed and grew an online information marketing publishing company from ground zero to over $1 million in sales in less than 12 months. Starting without a list, a product, a name or an offer, Heather Ann molded her client into a successful guru now known as an expert in his field.

Heather Ann has been named by a few as an 'Icon Creator' or the 'Wizard Behind the Curtain'. She has instructed, coached and promoted hundreds of entrepreneurs leading them down the path to success.

She has produced and managed over 350 seminars and events and hosted tele-seminars with many top online thought leaders such as Richard Flint, John Alanis, Susan Bratton, Alicia Lyttle, Tom Antion, Alex Mandossian, Legend

Joe Sugarman, Anthony Blake, David Lakhani, Robert Shemin and many others.

Heather Ann currently is the Author of…

Sexy Boss: How Female Entrepreneurs Are Beating the Big Boys; While Changing the Rule Book for Money, Success and Even Sex

and

The Game of Dating and How to Play it: A rule book for divorced men stepping back into the game.

Heather Ann Havenwood is smart, sexy, savvy and now stepping out from behind the curtain to educate, enlighten and empower women entrepreneurs to grow or start an online business and live a fearless and fulfilled life.

To Connect with Heather Ann:

Email: heather@sexybossinc.com

Facebook: www.Facebook.com/sexy.boss.inc

LinkedIn: www.HeatheronLinkedin.com

Sexy Boss Inc. Site www.sexybossinc.com

Twitter: www.Twitter.com/sexybossinc

Share This Book!

I mean it!

Tell your friends all about this book.

Share where you bought it.

Share it at lunch!

Share it at the gym!

Share it on the beach!

Share it on social media.

Share it using this hashtag...

#SexyBossBook